UK The classics Air Fryer Cookbook 2024

2800 Days Air Fryer Recipes Ingredient lists and nutritional information so you can make informed choices about your cuisine.

Doris D. Foster

Copyright © 2023 by Doris D. Foster- All rights reserved.

The content contained within this book may not be reproduced, duplicated, or transmitted without direct written permission from the author or the publisher. Under no circumstances will any blame or legal responsibility be held against the publisher, or author, for any damages, reparation, or monetary loss due to the information contained within this book, either directly or indirectly.

Legal Notice: This book is copyright protected. It is only for personal use. You cannot amend, distribute, sell, use, quote or paraphrase any part, or the content within this book, without the consent of the author or publisher.

Disclaimer Notice: Please note the information contained within this document is for educational and entertainment purposes only. All effort has been executed to present accurate, up to date, reliable, complete information. No warranties of any kind are declared or implied. Readers acknowledge that the author is not engaged in the rendering of legal, financial, medical, or professional advice. The content within this book has been derived from various sources. Please consult a licensed professional before attempting any techniques outlined in this book. By reading this document, the reader agrees that under no circumstances is the author responsible for any losses, direct or indirect, that are incurred as a result of the use of the information contained within this document, including, but not limited to, errors, omissions, or inaccuracies.

CONTENTS

An In-Depth Guide to Air Fryers 10
- The Advantages of Air Fryers 10
- Air Fryer Usage Tips 10
- Air Fryer Cleaning and Maintenance 11

Breakfast & Snacks And Fries Recipes 12
- Easy Cheese & Bacon Toasties 12
- Healthy Stuffed Peppers 12
- Tangy Breakfast Hash 13
- Hard Boiled Eggs Air Fryer Style 13
- Delicious Breakfast Casserole 14
- European Pancakes 14
- Easy Omelette 15
- Breakfast "pop Tarts" 15
- Crunchy Mexican Breakfast Wrap 16
- Egg & Bacon Breakfast Cups 16
- Mexican Breakfast Burritos 17

Sauces & Snack And Appetiser Recipes 17
- Sweet Potato Fries 17
- Air Fryer Turkey Avocado Burgers 18
- Ultra Crispy Air Fryer Chickpeas 18
- 2 Ingredient Air Fryer Pizza 19
- Roasted Almonds 19
- Air Fryer Stuffed Zucchini Boats With Sausage 20
- Popcorn Tofu 20
- Swede Fries 21
- Chicken & Bacon Parcels 21
- Air Fryer Hot Dogs 22

Beetroot Crisps 22

Air Fryer French Bread Pizza (homemade) 23

Pork Jerky 23

Cumin Shoestring Carrots 24

Potato Fries 24

Air Fryer Boiled Eggs 25

Cheesy Taco Crescents 25

Wholegrain Pitta Chips 26

Air Fryer Crispy Chickpeas 26

Garlic Cheese Bread 27

Corn Nuts 27

Muhammara 28

Poultry Recipes 28

Buffalo Wings 28

Air Fryer Frozen Chicken Cordon Bleu 29

Honey Cajun Chicken Thighs 29

Buffalo Chicken Wontons 30

Chicken And Cheese Chimichangas 30

Air Fryer Garlic Herb Turkey Breast 31

Turkey Cutlets In Mushroom Sauce 31

Healthy Air Fryer Herbed Turkey Breast With Lemon Pepper 32

Nashville Chicken 32

Pepper & Lemon Chicken Wings 33

Sticky Chicken Tikka Drumsticks 33

Olive Stained Turkey Breast 34

Cheddar & Bbq Stuffed Chicken 34

Air Fryer Hunters Chicken 35

Air Fryer Chicken Parmesan 35

Chicken Fried Rice 36

Chicken And Wheat Stir Fry 36

Garlic Parmesan Fried Chicken Wings 37

Air Fryer Chicken Wings 37

Chicken Tikka Masala 38

Smoky Chicken Breast 38

Air Fryer Chicken Strips 39

Beef & Lamb And Pork Recipes 39

Char Siu Buffalo 39

Homemade Crispy Pepperoni Pizza 40

Parmesan Crusted Pork Chops 40

Air Fryer Roast Pork Belly 41

Copycat Burger 41

Mediterranean Beef Meatballs 42

Air Fryer Pork Bratwurst 42

Butter Steak & Asparagus 43

Hamburgers 43

Salt And Pepper Belly Pork 44

Tender Ham Steaks 44

Pork Chilli Cheese Dogs 45

Beef Nacho Pinwheels 45

Vegetable & Beef Frittata 46

Cheesy Meatball Sub 46

Mustard Pork Tenderloin 47

Japanese Pork Chops 47

Beef Wellington 48

Chinese Chilli Beef 48

Honey & Mustard Meatballs 49

Air Fryer Breaded Pork Chops 49

Pork Taquitos 50

Fish & Seafood Recipes 50

- Peppery Lemon Shrimp 50
- Tilapia Fillets 51
- Chilli Lime Tilapia 51
- Copycat Fish Fingers 52
- Crispy Cajun Fish Fingers 52
- Air Fryer Tuna Mornay Parcels 53
- Air Fryer Spicy Bay Scallops 53
- Garlic Butter Salmon 54
- Salt & Pepper Calamari 54
- Sea Bass With Asparagus Spears 55
- Salmon Patties 55
- Alba Salad With Air Fried Butterfly Shrimp 56
- Extra Crispy Popcorn Shrimp 56
- Air Fryer Lemon Pepper Shrimp 57
- Tandoori Salmon 57
- Store-cupboard Fishcakes 58
- Air Fryer Salmon Fillets 58
- Honey Sriracha Salmon 59
- Air Fried Fish Tostadas With Mango Salsa 59
- Cajun Shrimp Boil 60
- Air Fryer Tuna 60
- Cajun Prawn Skewers 61

Side Dishes Recipes 61

- Garlic And Parsley Potatoes 61
- Sweet Potato Tots 62
- Zingy Roasted Carrots 62
- Grilled Bacon And Cheese 63

Potato Wedges 63

Orange Sesame Cauliflower 64

Bbq Beetroot Crisps 64

Stuffed Jacket Potatoes 65

Egg Fried Rice 65

Shishito Peppers 66

Potato Wedges With Rosemary 66

Air Fryer Eggy Bread 67

Crispy Cinnamon French Toast 67

Mexican Rice 68

Air Fryer Corn On The Cob 68

Roasted Okra 69

Pumpkin Fries 69

Courgette Gratin 70

Vegetarian & Vegan Recipes 70

Radish Hash Browns 70

Crispy Sweet & Spicy Cauliflower 71

Hasselback New Potatoes 71

Lentil Burgers 72

Roasted Brussels Sprouts 72

Roasted Cauliflower 73

Two-step Pizza 73

Bbq Soy Curls 74

Vegetarian Air Fryer Kimchi Bun 74

Roast Vegetables 75

Honey Roasted Parsnips 75

Pakoras 76

Baked Potato 76

Miso Mushrooms On Sourdough Toast 77

Flat Mushroom Pizzas ... 77

Air Fryer Carrots Recipes ... 78

Vegan Fried Ravioli ... 78

Quinoa-stuffed Romano Peppers ... 79

Air Fryer Cheese Sandwich ... 79

Air Fryer Muchrooms ... 80

Broccoli Cheese ... 80

Spanakopita Bites ... 81

Desserts Recipes ... 81

Banana Bread ... 81

Key Lime Cupcakes ... 82

Cherry Pies ... 82

Chonut Holes ... 83

Christmas Biscuits ... 83

Fried Oreos ... 84

Thai Fried Bananas ... 84

White Chocolate And Raspberry Loaf ... 85

Chocolate-glazed Banana Slices ... 85

Chocolate Dipped Biscuits ... 86

Melting Moments ... 86

Zebra Cake ... 87

Pecan & Molasses Flapjack ... 87

Lava Cakes ... 88

French Toast Sticks ... 88

Brownies ... 89

Mini Egg Buns ... 89

Lemon Buns ... 90

Strawberry Danish ... 90

Chocolate Orange Muffins ... 91

Grilled Ginger & Coconut Pineapple Rings 91

Recipe Index **92**

An In-Depth Guide to Air Fryers

Air fryers have revolutionized the way we cook by providing a healthier alternative to traditional deep frying. These compact kitchen appliances have gained immense popularity in recent years due to their ability to fry, bake, roast, and even grill with significantly less oil. In this comprehensive guide, we will explore the world of air fryers, covering their advantages, usage tips, and maintenance techniques.

The Advantages of Air Fryers

1 Healthier Cooking

One of the primary advantages of using an air fryer is its ability to cook food with minimal oil. Traditional deep frying involves submerging food in a large amount of hot oil, resulting in high calorie and fat content. Air fryers, on the other hand, use hot air circulation to crisp and brown the food, requiring only a fraction of the oil. This means you can enjoy your favorite fried foods with fewer calories and less saturated fat.

2 Versatility

Air fryers are incredibly versatile appliances that can handle a wide range of cooking tasks. From frying crispy French fries to roasting vegetables and even baking desserts, these machines can do it all. Some advanced models come with preset cooking functions, making it easy to prepare various dishes with just a push of a button.

3 Faster Cooking

Air fryers are known for their speed. The rapid circulation of hot air within the cooking chamber ensures that food cooks quickly and evenly. No more waiting for oil to heat up or dealing with unevenly cooked dishes. With an air fryer, you can have a meal ready in a fraction of the time it would take using conventional methods.

4 Easy Cleanup

Cleaning up after cooking can be a tedious task, but air fryers simplify the process. Most air fryer baskets and trays are non-stick and dishwasher safe, making cleanup a breeze. Additionally, since there's no splattering of hot oil, you won't have to deal with greasy stovetops or countertops.

Air Fryer Usage Tips

1 Preheat Your Air Fryer

To ensure even cooking and a crispy exterior, it's essential to preheat your air fryer before placing food inside. Preheating takes just a few minutes and sets the stage for perfectly cooked dishes.

2 Use the Right Amount of Oil

While air fryers require less oil than traditional frying, it's still important to use some oil to achieve that desired crispy texture. Use a cooking spray or a small amount of oil and evenly coat your food for the best results.

3 Avoid Overcrowding

Overcrowding the air fryer basket can lead to uneven cooking. Make sure there's enough space between food items to allow proper air circulation. If you have a large batch to cook, it's better to do it in multiple smaller batches.

4 Shake or Flip

For even cooking, remember to shake the basket or flip the food halfway through the cooking time. This ensures that all sides of your dish get that crispy finish.

5 Experiment with Recipes

Don't be afraid to experiment with different recipes in your air fryer. From chicken wings to vegetable skewers and even donuts, there are countless recipes available online that cater to air fryer cooking.

Air Fryer Cleaning and Maintenance

1 Regular Cleaning

Proper maintenance is essential to keep your air fryer running smoothly. After each use, allow the appliance to cool down, then remove the basket or tray and wash it with warm, soapy water. Wipe down the interior and exterior of the air fryer with a damp cloth. Make sure to clean the heating element and fan as well.

2 Dealing with Residue

If you notice stubborn residue or grease buildup, use a non-abrasive sponge or brush to gently scrub the affected areas. Avoid using metal utensils or abrasive cleaners, as they can damage the non-stick coating.

3 Filter Cleaning

Some air fryers come with removable filters to capture cooking odors and prevent them from lingering in your kitchen. These filters should be cleaned or replaced regularly according to the manufacturer's instructions.

4 Oil Tray Maintenance

Empty and clean the oil tray after each use to prevent the accumulation of excess oil and food particles. This helps maintain the efficiency of your air fryer and prevents smoke or unpleasant odors.

In conclusion, air fryers offer a healthier and more convenient way to enjoy fried and crispy dishes. Their versatility, speed, and easy maintenance make them a valuable addition to any kitchen. By following these usage tips and practicing proper cleaning and maintenance, you can make the most out of your air fryer and enjoy delicious meals with less guilt and hassle. Happy air frying!

Breakfast & Snacks And Fries Recipes

Easy Cheese & Bacon Toasties

Servings: 2

Ingredients:
- 4 slices of sandwich bread
- 2 slices of cheddar cheese
- 5 slices of pre-cooked bacon
- 1 tbsp melted butter
- 2 slices of mozzarella cheese

Directions:
1. Take the bread and spread the butter onto one side of each slice
2. Place one slice of bread into the fryer basket, buttered side facing downwards
3. Place the cheddar on top, followed by the bacon, mozzarella and the other slice of bread on top, buttered side upwards
4. Set your fryer to 170ºC
5. Cook for 4 minutes and then turn over and cook for another 3 minutes
6. Serve whilst still hot

Healthy Stuffed Peppers

Servings: 2

Ingredients:
- 1 large bell pepper, deseeded and cut into halves
- 1 tsp olive oil
- 4 large eggs
- Salt and pepper to taste

Directions:
1. Take your peppers and rub a little olive oil on the edges
2. Into each pepper, crack one egg and season with salt and pepper
3. You will need to insert a trivet into your air fryer to hold the peppers, and then arrange the peppers evenly
4. Set your fryer to 200ºC and cook for 13 minutes
5. Once cooked, remove and serve with a little more seasoning, if required

Tangy Breakfast Hash

Servings: 6

Ingredients:
- 2 tbsp olive oil
- 2 sweet potatoes, cut into cubes
- 1 tbsp smoked paprika
- 1 tsp salt
- 1 tsp black pepper
- 2 slices of bacon, cut into small pieces

Directions:
1. Preheat your air fryer to 200°C
2. Pour the olive oil into a large mixing bowl
3. Add the bacon, seasonings, potatoes and toss to evenly coat
4. Transfer the mixture into the air fryer and cook for 12-16 minutes
5. Stir after 10 minutes and continue to stir periodically for another 5 minutes

Hard Boiled Eggs Air Fryer Style

Servings: 2

Ingredients:
- 4 large eggs
- 1 tsp cayenne pepper
- Salt and pepper for seasoning

Directions:
1. Preheat the air fryer to 220°C
2. Take a wire rack and place inside the air fryer
3. Lay the eggs on the rack
4. Cook for between 15-17 minutes, depending upon how you like your eggs
5. Remove from the fryer and place in a bowl of cold water for around 5 minutes
6. Peel and season with the cayenne and the salt and pepper

Delicious Breakfast Casserole

Servings: 4

Ingredients:

- 4 frozen hash browns
- 8 sausages, cut into pieces
- 4 eggs
- 1 diced yellow pepper
- 1 diced green pepper
- 1 diced red pepper
- Half a diced onion

Directions:

1. Line the bottom of your fryer with aluminium foil and arrange the hash browns inside
2. Add the sausage on top (uncooked)
3. Now add the onions and the peppers, sprinkling evenly
4. Cook the casserole on 170ºC for around 10 minutes
5. Open your fryer and give the mixture a good stir
6. Combine the eggs in a small bowl and pour over the casserole, closing the lid
7. Cook for another 10 minutes on the same temperature
8. Serve with a little seasoning to taste

European Pancakes

Servings: 5

Ingredients:

- 3 large eggs
- 130g flour
- 140ml whole milk
- 2 tbsp unsweetened apple sauce
- A pinch of salt

Directions:

1. Set your fryer to 200ºC and add five ramekins inside to heat up
2. Place all your ingredients inside a blender to combine
3. Spray the ramekins with a little cooking spray
4. Pour the batter into the ramekins carefully
5. Fry for between 6-8 minutes, depending on your preference
6. Serve with your favourite toppings

Easy Omelette

Servings: 1

Ingredients:
- 50ml milk
- 2 eggs
- 60g grated cheese, any you like
- Any garnishes you like, such as mushrooms, peppers, etc.

Directions:
1. Take a small mixing bowl and crack the eggs inside, whisking with the milk
2. Add the salt and garnishes and combine again
3. Grease a 6x3" pan and pour the mixture inside
4. Arrange the pan inside the air fryer basket
5. Cook at 170°C for 10 minutes
6. At the halfway point, sprinkle the cheese on top
7. Loosen the edges with a spatula before serving

Breakfast "pop Tarts"

Servings: 6

Ingredients:
- 2 slices of prepared pie crust, shortbread or filo will work fine
- 2 tbsp strawberry jam
- 60ml plain yogurt
- 1 tsp cornstarch
- 1 tsp Stevia sweetener
- 2 tbsp cream cheese
- A drizzle of olive oil

Directions:
1. Lay your pie crust flat and cut into 6 separate rectangular pieces
2. In a small bowl, mix together the cornstarch and the jam
3. Spread 1 tablespoon of the mixture on top of the crust
4. Fold each crust over to form the tart
5. Seal down the edges using a fork
6. Arrange your tarts inside the frying basket and spray with a little olive oil
7. Heat to 175°C and cook for 10 minutes
8. Meanwhile, combine the yogurt, cream cheese and Stevia in a bowl
9. Remove the tarts and allow to cool
10. Once cool, add the frosting on top and sprinkle with the sugar sprinkles

Crunchy Mexican Breakfast Wrap

Servings: 2

Ingredients:
- 2 large tortillas
- 2 corn tortillas
- 1 sliced jalapeño pepper
- 4 tbsp ranchero sauce
- 1 sliced avocado
- 25g cooked pinto beans

Directions:
1. Take each of your large tortillas and add the egg, jalapeño, sauce, the corn tortillas, the avocado and the pinto beans, in that order. If you want to add more sauce at this point, you can
2. Fold over your wrap to make sure that nothing escapes
3. Place each wrap into your fryer and cook at 190°C for 6 minutes
4. Remove your wraps and place in the oven, cooking for a further 5 minutes at 180°C, until crispy
5. Place each wrap into a frying pan and crisp a little more on a low heat, for a couple of minutes on each side

Egg & Bacon Breakfast Cups

Servings: 8

Ingredients:
- 6 eggs
- 1 chopped red pepper
- 1 chopped green pepper
- 1 chopped yellow pepper
- 2 tbsp double cream
- 50g chopped spinach
- 50g grated cheddar cheese
- 50g grated mozzarella cheese
- 3 slices of cooked bacon, crumbled into pieces

Directions:
1. Take a large mixing bowl and crack the eggs
2. Add the cream and season with a little salt and pepper, combining everything well
3. Add the peppers, spinach, onions, both cheeses, and the crumbled bacon, combining everything once more
4. You will need silicone moulds or cups for this part, and you should pour equal amounts of the mixture into 8 cups
5. Cook at 150°C for around 12 or 15 minutes, until the eggs are cooked properly

Mexican Breakfast Burritos

Servings: 6

Ingredients:
- 6 scrambled eggs
- 6 medium tortillas
- Half a minced red pepper
- 8 sausages, cut into cubes and browned
- 4 pieces of bacon, pre-cooked and cut into pieces
- 65g grated cheese of your choice
- A small amount of olive oil for cooking

Directions:
1. Into a regular mixing bowl, combine the eggs, bell pepper, bacon pieces, the cheese, and the browned sausage, giving everything a good stir
2. Take your first tortilla and place half a cup of the mixture into the middle, folding up the top and bottom and rolling closed
3. Repeat until all your tortillas have been used
4. Arrange the burritos into the bottom of your fryer and spray with a little oil
5. Cook the burritos at 170ºC for 5 minutes

Sauces & Snack And Appetiser Recipes

Sweet Potato Fries

Servings: 4

Ingredients:
- 2 medium sweet potatoes
- 2 teaspoons olive oil
- ½ teaspoon salt
- ½ teaspoon chilli/hot red pepper flakes
- ½ teaspoon smoked paprika

Directions:
1. Preheat the air-fryer to 190ºC/375ºF.
2. Peel the sweet potatoes and slice into fries about 1 x 1 cm/½ x ½ in. by the length of the potato. Toss the sweet potato fries in the oil, salt, chilli and paprika, making sure every fry is coated.
3. Tip into the preheated air-fryer in a single layer (you may need to cook them in two batches, depending on the size of your air-fryer). Air-fry for 10 minutes, turning once halfway during cooking. Serve immediately.

Air Fryer Turkey Avocado Burgers

Servings: 4
Cooking Time: 15 Mints
Ingredients:
- 454 g ground turkey
- 2 cloves garlic , minced
- 1 Tablespoon Worcestershire , fish sauce, or soy sauce (fish sauce is our favorite)
- 1 teaspoon dried herbs (oregano, thyme, dill, basil, marjoram)
- 80 g minced fresh onion
- 1/2 teaspoon salt , or to taste
- Lots of black pepper
- oil spray , for coating
- BURGER ASSEMBLY:
- 4 Buns
- 1 avocado , sliced
- Optional: cheese, radish sprouts, lettuce, tomato, et

Directions:
1. Preheat air fryer at 380°F/193°C for 5 minutes.
2. In bowl, combine turkey, garlic, Worcestershire sauce (or fish sauce or soy sauce), dried herbs, onion, salt and pepper. Mix everything until just combined.
3. Divide and flatten into 4 patties about 4" wide. Spray both sides with oil. If you have a smaller air fryer, you'll have to cook in two batches.
4. Air Fry at 380°F/193°C for 10-12 minutes, flip after 6 minutes. Cook to your preference or until the internal temperature reaches 165°F/74°C. If your patty is thicker, you many need to cook for a few more minutes.
5. For Turkey Cheeseburgers: add the slices of cheese on top of the cooked patties. Air fry at 380°F/193°C for about 30 seconds to 1 minute to melt the cheese.
6. For best juiciness, cover the patties and let rest for 3 minutes. Warm the buns in the air fryer at 380°F/193°C for about 1 minute while patties are resting. Serve on buns, topped with 1/4 avocado and your favorite burger toppings

Ultra Crispy Air Fryer Chickpeas

Servings: 2
Cooking Time: 15 Mints
Ingredients:
- 250 g can of chickpeas (drained and rinsed)
- 1 tablespoon olive oil
- ⅛ teaspoon salt
- ¼ teaspoon garlic powder
- ¼ teaspoon onion powder
- ½ teaspoon paprika

Directions:
1. Heat air fryer to 200°C/400° .
2. Drain and rinse chickpeas (no need to dry). Toss with olive oil and spices.
3. Dump the whole batch of chickpeas in the air fryer basket. Cook for 12-15 minutes, shaking a couple of times.
4. When chickpeas are cooked to your liking, remove from air fryer, taste and add more salt and pepper to taste.
5. Store in an open container.

2 Ingredient Air Fryer Pizza

Servings: 2-4
Cooking Time: 10 Mints

Ingredients:

- 240 g/1 cup natural or Greek yoghurt
- 350 g/2 cups self-raising flour
- grated cheese
- pizza sauce/passata
- toppings of your choice (pepperoni, pineapple, peppers, chicken etc)

Directions:

1. Mix the self-raising flour and yoghurt together until a dough consistency has been formed.
2. Split dough in
3. Roll each one out on a floured surface.
4. Place on a bit of parchment paper in an air fryer basket and cook at 200°C/400°F for 8 to 10 minutes, turning over half way.
5. Take pizza out and add pizza sauce, grated cheese & any other toppings of your choice.
6. Return to the air fryer basket and cook for a further 3 minutes.
7. Repeat with the 2nd pizza.

Roasted Almonds

Servings: 2

Ingredients:

- 1 tbsp soy sauce
- 1 tbsp garlic powder
- 1 tsp paprika
- ¼ tsp pepper
- 400g raw almonds

Directions:

1. Place all of the ingredients apart from the almonds in a bowl and mix
2. Add the almonds and coat well
3. Place the almonds in the air fryer and cook at 160°C for 6 minutes shaking every 2 minutes

Air Fryer Stuffed Zucchini Boats With Sausage

Servings: 4
Cooking Time: 10 Mints

Ingredients:

- 2 medium zucchini, halved and cored
- 227 g uncooked sausage meat
- 60 ml breadcrumbs
- 57 g grated cheese
- 2 Tablespoons fresh chopped parsley
- oil spray, for coating

Directions:

1. Halve and core the zucchini.
2. Lay zucchini cut-side down and spray skin side with olive oil spray.
3. Flip the zucchini and stuff the center with sausage. Top with breadcrumbs and cheese. Spray tops with oil spray.
4. Lay zucchini in air fryer making sure the zucchini doesn't tip over (see note below).
5. Air Fry at 360°F/180°C for 10-14 minutes or until sausage is cooked all the way through. Serve with sauce if you want. Top with parsley. It's delicious either way!

Popcorn Tofu

Servings: 4

Ingredients:

- 400g firm tofu
- 100g chickpea flour
- 100g oatmeal
- 2 tbsp yeast
- 150ml milk
- 400g breadcrumbs
- 1 tsp garlic powder
- 1 tsp onion powder
- 1 tbsp dijon mustard
- ½ tsp salt
- ½ tsp pepper
- 2 tbsp vegetable bouillon

Directions:

1. Rip the tofu into pieces. Place the breadcrumbs into a bowl, in another bowl mix the remaining ingredients
2. Dip the tofu into the batter mix and then dip into the breadcrumbs
3. Heat the air fryer to 175ºC
4. Place the tofu in the air fryer and cook for 12 minutes shaking halfway through

Swede Fries

Servings: 4

Ingredients:
- 1 medium swede/rutabaga
- ½ teaspoon salt
- ½ teaspoon freshly ground black pepper
- 1½ teaspoons dried thyme
- 1 tablespoon olive oil

Directions:
1. Preheat the air-fryer to 160°C/325°F.
2. Peel the swede/rutabaga and slice into fries about 6 x 1 cm/2½ x ½ in., then toss the fries in the salt, pepper, thyme and oil, making sure every fry is coated.
3. Tip into the preheated air-fryer in a single layer (you may need to cook them in two batches, depending on the size of your air-fryer) and air-fry for 15 minutes, shaking the drawer halfway through. Then increase the temperature to 180°C/350°F and cook for a further 5 minutes. Serve immediately.

Chicken & Bacon Parcels

Servings: 4

Ingredients:
- 2 chicken breasts, boneless and skinless
- 200ml BBQ sauce
- 7 slices of bacon, cut lengthwise into halves
- 2 tbsp brown sugar

Directions:
1. Preheat the air fryer to 220°C
2. Cut the chicken into strips, you should have 7 in total
3. Wrap two strips of the bacon around each piece of chicken
4. Brush the BBQ sauce over the top and sprinkle with the brown sugar
5. Place the chicken into the basket and cook for 5 minutes
6. Turn the chicken over and cook for another 5 minutes

Air Fryer Hot Dogs

Servings: 6
Cooking Time: 5 Mints
Ingredients:
- 6 hot dogs
- 6 hot dog buns

Directions:
1. Place hot dogs in basket of air fryer. Cook at 200°C/400°F for 4 minutes. Remove from basket.
2. Place buns in basket and cook at 200°C/400°F.
3. Place hot dogs in buns and top with desired toppings

Beetroot Crisps

Servings: 2
Ingredients:
- 3 medium beetroots
- 2 tbsp oil
- Salt to taste

Directions:
1. Peel and thinly slice the beetroot
2. Coat with the oil and season with salt
3. Preheat the air fryer to 200°C
4. Place in the air fryer and cook for 12-18 minutes until crispy

Air Fryer French Bread Pizza (homemade)

Servings: 2
Cooking Time: 10 Mints
Ingredients:
- 1 French bread loaf
- 1/2 cup (120 ml) pizza sauce or tomato sauce
- 1/3 cup (40 g) shredded cheese
- salt , to taste
- black pepper, to taste

Directions:
1. Cut French bread loaf to fit the length of your air fryer. Slice in half lengthwise.
2. Lightly spray both sides for an extra crispy crust. Place in air fryer basket/tray with the bottom (crust) side up (only cook in a single layer – cook the pizzas in batches if needed). Air Fry at 360°F/182°C about 2 minutes.
3. Flip the bread, add sauce & toppings.
4. Cover toppings with an air fryer rack to keep toppings from flying around.
5. Air Fry 360°F/182°C for 2-4 minutes or until heated through and cheese is melted. Try air frying for about 2 minutes first. If you want the top to be crispier, add an additional minute or two until the pizza is crispy and cheese is melted.
6. Allow pizza to cool for about 2 minutes. Serve warm.

Pork Jerky

Servings: 35
Ingredients:
- 300g mince pork
- 1 tbsp oil
- 1 tbsp sriracha
- 1 tbsp soy
- ½ tsp pink curing salt
- 1 tbsp rice vinegar
- ½ tsp salt
- ½ tsp pepper
- ½ tsp onion powder

Directions:
1. Mix all ingredients in a bowl until combined
2. Refrigerate for about 8 hours
3. Shape into sticks and place in the air fryer
4. Heat the air fryer to 160ºC
5. Cook for 1 hour turn then cook for another hour
6. Turn again and cook for another hour
7. Cover with paper and sit for 8 hours

Cumin Shoestring Carrots

Servings: 2

Ingredients:
- 300 g/10½ oz. carrots
- 1 teaspoon cornflour/cornstarch
- 1 teaspoon ground cumin
- ¼ teaspoon salt
- 1 tablespoon olive oil
- garlic mayonnaise, to serve

Directions:
1. Preheat the air-fryer to 200ºC/400ºF.
2. Peel the carrots and cut into thin fries, roughly 10 cm x 1 cm x 5 mm/4 x ½ x ¼ in. Toss the carrots in a bowl with all the other ingredients.
3. Add the carrots to the preheated air-fryer and air-fry for 9 minutes, shaking the drawer of the air-fryer a couple of times during cooking. Serve with garlic mayo on the side.

Potato Fries

Servings: 2

Ingredients:
- 2 large potatoes (baking potato size)
- 1 teaspoon olive oil
- salt

Directions:
1. Peel the potatoes and slice into fries about 5 x 1.5cm/¾ x ¾ in. by the length of the potato. Submerge the fries in a bowl of cold water and place in the fridge for about 10 minutes.
2. Meanwhile, preheat the air-fryer to 160ºC/325ºF.
3. Drain the fries thoroughly, then toss in the oil and season. Tip into the preheated air-fryer in a single layer (you may need to cook them in two batches, depending on the size of your air-fryer). Air-fry for 15 minutes, tossing once during cooking by shaking the air-fryer drawer, then increase the temperature of the air-fryer to 200ºC/400ºF and cook for a further 3 minutes. Serve immediately.

Air Fryer Boiled Eggs

Servings: 2-4
Cooking Time: 10 Mints
Ingredients:
- 4 eggs (cook as many as you need)

Directions:
1. Add room temperature eggs to the basket of your air fryer, and leave some space between them so that there is room for the hot air to circulate. Use a metal rack if needed to fit more in.
2. Set the air fryer temperature at 150°C/300°F. Cook according to how well you want your eggs (starting at 8 minutes for runny, up to 12 minutes for hard boiled).
3. At the end of the cooking time remove from the air fryer basket and plunge into an ice bath or into a bowl of cold water – this will prevent the eggs from continuing to cook.
4. Once they have cooled down a little and can be handled, remove the shell.

Cheesy Taco Crescents

Servings: 8
Ingredients:
- 1 can Pillsbury crescent sheets, or alternative
- 4 Monterey Jack cheese sticks
- 150g browned minced beef
- ½ pack taco seasoning mix

Directions:
1. Preheat the air fryer to 200°C
2. Combine the minced beef and the taco seasoning, warm in the microwave for about 2 minutes
3. Cut the crescent sheets into 8 equal squares
4. Cut the cheese sticks in half
5. Add half a cheese stick to each square, and 2 tablespoons of mince
6. Roll up the dough and pinch at the ends to seal
7. Place in the air fryer and cook for 5 minutes
8. Turnover and cook for another 3 minutes

Wholegrain Pitta Chips

Servings: 2

Ingredients:
- 2 round wholegrain pittas, chopped into quarters
- 1 teaspoon olive oil
- ½ teaspoon garlic salt

Directions:
1. Preheat the air-fryer to 200°C/400°F.
2. Pop the pittas into the preheated air-fryer and air-fry for 1 minute.
3. Remove the pittas from the air-fryer and spread a layer of the passata/strained tomatoes on the pittas, then scatter over the mozzarella, oregano and oil. Return to the air-fryer and air-fry for a further 4 minutes. Scatter over the basil leaves and serve immediately.

Air Fryer Crispy Chickpeas

Servings: 3-4
Cooking Time: 15-20 Mints

Ingredients:
- 1 can Chickpeas
- Olive Oil
- Salt
- Chili powder
- Za'atar (Thyme, Cumin, Coriander, Sesame Seeds, Sumac, Chili fla

Directions:
1. Drain and rinse the chickpeas, put them on a paper towel and leave to dry for about 10 minutes.
2. Transfer the chickpeas to a bowl, drizzle with oil and add spices. Shake until evenly distributed.
3. Transfer to the air fryer basket, set to 200°C/400°F for 12-15 minutes (keep an eye on them from about 12 minutes).
4. Enjoy!

Garlic Cheese Bread

Servings: 2

Ingredients:

- 250g grated mozzarella
- 50g grated parmesan
- 1 egg
- ½ tsp garlic powder

Directions:

1. Line air fryer with parchment paper
2. Mix ingredients in a bowl
3. Press into a circle onto the parchment paper in the air fryer
4. Heat the air fryer to 175°C
5. Cook for 10 minutes

Corn Nuts

Servings: 8

Ingredients:

- 1 giant white corn
- 3 tbsp vegetable oil
- 2 tsp salt

Directions:

1. Place the corn in a large bowl, cover with water and sit for 8 hours
2. Drain, pat dry and air dry for 20 minutes
3. Preheat the air fryer to 200°C
4. Place in a bowl and coat with oil and salt
5. Cook in the air fryer for 10 minutes shake then cook for a further 10 minutes

Muhammara

Servings: 4

Ingredients:
- 4 romano peppers
- 4 tablespoons olive oil
- 100 g/1 cup walnuts
- 90 g/1 heaped cup dried breadcrumbs
- 1 teaspoon cumin
- 2 tablespoons pomegranate molasses
- freshly squeezed juice of ½ a lemon
- ½ teaspoon chilli/chili salt (or salt and some chilli/hot red pepper flakes combined)
- fresh pomegranate seeds, to serve

Directions:
1. Preheat the air-fryer to 180ºC/350ºF.
2. Rub the peppers with ½ teaspoon of the olive oil. Add the peppers to the preheated air-fryer and air-fry for 8 minutes.
3. Meanwhile, lightly toast the walnuts by tossing them in a shallow pan over a medium heat for 3–5 minutes. Allow to cool, then grind the walnuts in a food processor. Once the peppers are cooked, chop off the tops and discard most of the seeds. Add to the food processor with all other ingredients. Process until smooth. Allow to cool in the fridge, then serve the dip with pomegranate seeds on top.

Poultry Recipes
Buffalo Wings

Servings: 4

Ingredients:
- 500g chicken wings
- 1 tbsp olive oil
- 5 tbsp cayenne pepper sauce
- 75g butter
- 2 tbsp vinegar
- 1 tsp garlic powder
- ¼ tsp cayenne pepper

Directions:
1. Preheat the air fryer to 182C
2. Take a large mixing bowl and add the chicken wings
3. Drizzle oil over the wings, coating evenly
4. Cook for 25 minutes and then flip the wings and cook for 5 more minutes
5. In a saucepan over a medium heat, mix the hot pepper sauce, butter, vinegar, garlic powder and cayenne pepper, combining well
6. Pour the sauce over the wings and flip to coat, before serving

Air Fryer Frozen Chicken Cordon Bleu

Servings: 1
Cooking Time: 15 Mints

Ingredients:
- 1 frozen chicken cordon bleu

Directions:
1. Preheat air fryer to 180°C/350°F, for approximately 2-3 minutes.
2. Place frozen chicken cordon bleu in an air fryer basket. If you are cooking more than one, ensure they are not touching.
3. Air fry cordon bleu for: 15-20 minutes for frozen pre-cooked cordon bleu, or - 30-35 minutes for frozen raw cordon bleu See note 2.
4. When cooking time is up, check internal temperature to make sure cordon bleu have reached at least 74°C/165°F in the center of the thickest part. If required, air fry for additional 2-3 minute intervals until the correct temperature is reached

Honey Cajun Chicken Thighs

Servings: 6

Ingredients:
- 100ml buttermilk
- 1 tsp hot sauce
- 400g skinless, boneless chicken thighs
- 150g all purpose flour
- 60g tapioca flour
- 2.5 tsp cajun seasoning
- ½ tsp garlic salt
- ½ tsp honey powder
- ¼ tsp ground paprika
- ⅛ tsp cayenne pepper
- 4 tsp honey

Directions:
1. Take a large bowl and combine the buttermilk and hot sauce
2. Transfer to a plastic bag and add the chicken thighs
3. Allow to marinate for 30 minutes
4. Take another bowl and add the flour, tapioca flour, cajun seasoning, garlic, salt, honey powder, paprika, and cayenne pepper, combining well
5. Dredge the chicken through the mixture
6. Preheat the air fryer to 175C
7. Cook for 15 minutes before flipping the thighs over and cooking for another 10 minutes
8. Drizzle 1 tsp of honey over each thigh

Buffalo Chicken Wontons

Servings: 6

Ingredients:
- 200g shredded chicken
- 1 tbsp buffalo sauce
- 4 tbsp softened cream cheese
- 1 sliced spring onion
- 2 tbsp blue cheese crumbles
- 12 wonton wrappers

Directions:
1. Preheat the air fryer to 200ºC
2. Take a bowl and combine the chicken and buffalo sauce
3. In another bowl mix the cream cheese until a smooth consistency has formed and then combine the scallion blue cheese and seasoned chicken
4. Take the wonton wrappers and run wet fingers along each edge
5. Place 1 tbsp of the filling into the centre of the wonton and fold the corners together
6. Cook at 200ºC for 3 to 5 minutes, until golden brown

Chicken And Cheese Chimichangas

Servings: 6

Ingredients:
- 100g shredded chicken (cooked)
- 150g nacho cheese
- 1 chopped jalapeño pepper
- 6 flour tortillas
- 5 tbsp salsa
- 60g refried beans
- 1 tsp cumin
- 0.5 tsp chill powder
- Salt and pepper to taste

Directions:
1. Take a large mixing bowl and add all of the ingredients, combining well
2. Add ⅓ of the filling to each tortilla and roll into a burrito shape
3. Spray the air fryer with cooking spray and heat to 200ºC
4. Place the chimichangas in the air fryer and cook for 7 minutes

Air Fryer Garlic Herb Turkey Breast

Servings: 6
Cooking Time: 10 Mints
Ingredients:
- 900 g turkey breast, skin on
- Salt
- Freshlyground black pepper
- 57 g/4 tbsp. butter, melted
- 3 cloves garlic, crushed
- 1 tsp. freshly chopped thyme
- 1 tsp. freshly chopped rosemary

Directions:
1. Pat turkey breast dry and season on both sides with salt and pepper.
2. In a small bowl, combine melted butter, garlic, thyme, and rosemary. Brush butter all over turkey breast.
3. Place in basket of air fryer, skin side up and cook at 190°C/375°F for 40 minutes or until internal temperature reaches 73°C/165°F, flipping halfway through.
4. Let rest for 5 minutes before slicing

Turkey Cutlets In Mushroom Sauce

Servings: 2
Ingredients:
- 2 turkey cutlets
- 1 tbsp butter
- 1 can of cream of mushroom sauce
- 160ml milk
- Salt and pepper for seasoning

Directions:
1. Preheat the air fryer to 220°C
2. Brush the turkey cults with the butter and seasoning
3. Place in the air fryer and cook for 11 minutes
4. Add the mushroom soup and milk to a pan and cook over the stone for around 10 minutes, stirring every so often
5. Top the turkey cutlets with the sauce

Healthy Air Fryer Herbed Turkey Breast With Lemon Pepper

Servings: 6
Cooking Time: 55 Mints

Ingredients:

- 1360 g de-boned uncooked turkey breast *see recipe head note
- 2 Tablespoons oil
- 1 Tablespoon Worcestershire sauce
- 1 teaspoon lemon pepper or dried herb seasoning
- 1/2 teaspoon salt , or to taste

Directions:

1. Make sure the turkey breast is completely thawed or else it will not cook through. Pat the turkey dry.
2. In a bowl or plastic bag, combine the oil, Worcestershire sauce, lemon pepper or herbs, and salt. Add the turkey to the marinade, making sure the marinade completely coats the turkey breast. If possible, marinate for 1-2 hours.
3. Lightly spray or rub oil on the air fryer basket. Remove the turkey from the marinade and place the turkey breast skin-side down in the air fryer basket.
4. Air Fry at 350°F/175°C for 25 minutes. Flip the turkey breast to skin side up, and Air Fry for another 25-35 minutes until internal temperature of turkey reaches 165°F in the thickest part. If you're cooking bone-in turkey breast, cook for additional 5-10 minutes if needed.
5. Allow the breast to rest for 5 minutes. Slice and serve while warm.

Nashville Chicken

Servings: 4

Ingredients:

- 400g boneless chicken breast tenders
- 2 tsp salt
- 2 tsp coarsely ground black pepper
- 2 tbsp hot sauce
- 2 tbsp pickle juice
- 500g all purpose flour
- 3 large eggs
- 300ml buttermilk
- 2 tbsp olive oil
- 6 tbsp cayenne pepper
- 3 tbsp dark brown sugar
- 1 tsp chilli powder
- 1 tsp garlic powder
- 1 tsp paprika
- Salt and pepper to taste

Directions:

1. Take a large mixing bowl and add the chicken, hot sauce, pickle juice, salt and pepper and combine
2. Place in the refrigerator for 3 hours
3. Transfer the flour to a bowl
4. Take another bowl and add the eggs, buttermilk and 1 tbsp of the hot sauce, combining well
5. Press each piece of chicken into the flour and coat well
6. Place the chicken into the buttermilk mixture and then back into the flour
7. Allow to sit or 10 minutes
8. Preheat the air fryer to 193C
9. Whisk together the spices, brown sugar and olive oil to make the sauce and pour over the chicken tenders
10. Serve whilst still warm

Pepper & Lemon Chicken Wings

Servings: 2

Ingredients:
- 1kg chicken wings
- 1/4 tsp cayenne pepper
- 2 tsp lemon pepper seasoning
- 3 tbsp butter
- 1 tsp honey
- An extra 1 tsp lemon pepper seasoning for the sauce

Directions:
1. Preheat the air fryer to 260°C
2. Place the lemon pepper seasoning and cayenne in a bowl and combine
3. Coat the chicken in the seasoning
4. Place the chicken in the air fryer and cook for 20 minutes, turning over halfway
5. Turn the temperature up to 300°C and cook for another 6 minutes
6. Meanwhile, melt the butter and combine with the honey and the rest of the seasoning
7. Remove the wings from the air fryer and pour the sauce over the top

Sticky Chicken Tikka Drumsticks

Servings: 4

Ingredients:
- 12 chicken drumsticks
- MARINADE
- 100 g/½ cup Greek yogurt
- 2 tablespoons tikka paste
- 2 teaspoons ginger preserve
- freshly squeezed juice of ½ a lemon
- ¾ teaspoon salt

Directions:
1. Make slices across each of the drumsticks with a sharp knife. Mix the marinade ingredients together in a bowl, then add the drumsticks. Massage the marinade into the drumsticks, then leave to marinate in the fridge overnight or for at least 6 hours.
2. Preheat the air-fryer to 200°C/400°F.
3. Lay the drumsticks on an air-fryer liner or a piece of pierced parchment paper. Place the paper and drumsticks in the preheated air-fryer. Air-fry for 6 minutes, then turn over and cook for a further 6 minutes. Check the internal temperature of the drumsticks has reached at least 75°C/167°F using a meat thermometer – if not, cook for another few minutes and then serve.

Olive Stained Turkey Breast

Servings: 14

Ingredients:
- The brine from a can of olives
- 150ml buttermilk
- 300g boneless and skinless turkey breasts
- 1 sprig fresh rosemary
- 2 sprigs fresh thyme

Directions:
1. Take a mixing bowl and combine the olive brine and buttermilk
2. Pour the mixture over the turkey breast
3. Add the rosemary and thyme sprigs
4. Place into the refrigerator for 8 hours
5. Remove from the fridge and let the turkey reach room temperature
6. Preheat the air fryer to 175C
7. Cook for 15 minutes, ensuring the turkey is cooked through before serving

Cheddar & Bbq Stuffed Chicken

Servings: 2

Ingredients:
- 3 strips of bacon
- 100g cheddar cheese
- 3 tbsp barbecue sauce
- 300g skinless and boneless chicken breasts
- salt and ground pepper to taste

Directions:
1. Preheat the air fryer to 190°C
2. Cook one of the back strips for 2 minutes, before cutting into small pieces
3. Increase the temperature of the air fryer to 200°C
4. Mix together the cooked bacon, cheddar cheese and 1 tbsp barbecue sauce
5. Take the chicken and make a pouch by cutting a 1 inch gap into the top
6. Stuff the pouch with the bacon and cheese mixture and then wrap around the chicken breast
7. Coat the chicken with the rest of the BBQ sauce
8. Cook for 10 minutes in the air fryer, before turning and cooking for an additional 10 minutes

Air Fryer Hunters Chicken

Servings: 4-6
Cooking Time: 20 Mints

Ingredients:
- Spray oil
- 2 Chicken breasts
- 4 pieces of smoked streaky bacon
- 40 g grated cheddar or mozzarella / cheddar mix
- 50 ml BBQ sauce

Directions:
1. Season your chicken breasts well.
2. Lightly spray the chicken breasts with a little oil.
3. Cook at 200°C/400°F for 10 minutes.
4. Wrap each chicken breast with two pieces of streaky bacon.
5. Cook at 200°C/400°F for 6 minutes.
6. Spread on the BBQ sauce and add the grated cheddar carefully.
7. Cook at 200°C/400°F for another 4-5 minutes.
8. Check the temperature of your air fryer hunters chicken before serving, to ensure it is a minimum of 74°C/165°F internally.

Air Fryer Chicken Parmesan

Servings: 4
Cooking Time: 10 Mints

Ingredients:
- 2 large boneless chicken breasts
- Salt
- Freshlyground black pepper
- 40 g plain flour
- 2 large eggs
- 100 g panko bread crumbs
- 25 g freshly grated Parmesan
- 1 tsp. dried oregano
- 1/2 tsp.
- garlic powder
- 1/2 tsp. chilli flakes
- 240 g marinara/tomato sauce
- 100 g grated mozzarella
- Freshly chopped parsley, for garnish

Directions:
1. Pat the skin of your chicken dry and using a knife make small holes all around the chicken.
2. In a blender combine all remaining ingredients and blend for three minutes. Pour half the jerk marinade over the chicken and massage it in. Refrigerate overnight.
3. When ready to cook, bring grill temperature up to 165°C/330°F. Place the chicken skin side down and close BBQ lid for 5-7 minutes until it starts to brown. Turn over and cook for the remaining 5-7 minutes. Repeat twice more until chicken is dark brown and cooked all the way through.
4. Move chicken to the sides of the grill and brush remaining jerk sauce on top. Close the lid and cook for a further 5-7minutes.
5. Remove from BBQ and leave chicken to cool for around 10 minutes. Either eat on the bone or chop the meat into smaller pieces and serve.

Chicken Fried Rice

Servings: 4

Ingredients:

- 400g cooked white rice
- 400g cooked chicken, diced
- 200g frozen peas and carrots
- 6 tbsp soy sauce
- 1 tbsp vegetable oil
- 1 diced onion

Directions:

1. Take a large bowl and add the rice, vegetable oil and soy sauce and combine well
2. Add the frozen peas, carrots, diced onion and the chicken and mix together well
3. Pour the mixture into a nonstick pan
4. Place the pan into the air fryer
5. Cook at 182C for 20 minutes

Chicken And Wheat Stir Fry

Servings: 4

Ingredients:

- 1 onion
- 1 clove of garlic
- 200g skinless boneless chicken breast halves
- 3 whole tomatoes
- 400ml water
- 1 chicken stock cube
- 1 tbsp curry powder
- 130g wheat berries
- 1 tbsp vegetable oil

Directions:

1. Thinly slice the onion and garlic
2. Chop the chicken and tomatoes into cubes
3. Take a large saucepan and add the water, chicken stock, curry powder and wheat berries, combining well
4. Pour the oil into the air fryer bowl and heat for 5 minutes at 200°C
5. Add the remaining ingredients and pour the contents into the air fryer
6. Cook for 15 minutes

Garlic Parmesan Fried Chicken Wings

Servings: 4

Ingredients:
- 16 chicken wing drumettes
- Cooking spray
- 240ml low fat buttermilk
- 150g flour
- 140g grated parmesan
- 2 tbsp low sodium soy sauce
- 1 sachet of your favourite chicken seasoning
- 1 tsp garlic powder
- Salt and pepper to taste

Directions:
1. Place the chicken onto a cooking tray and pour the soy sauce over the top, ensuring it is fully coated
2. Season the chicken and place in the refrigerator for 30 minutes
3. Add the flour and parmesan into a ziplock bag
4. Coat the chicken with buttermilk and add it to the ziplock bag with the flour
5. Preheat your air fryer to 200°C
6. Place the chicken into the air fryer for 20 minutes
7. Shake the air fryer basket every 5 minutes until the 20 minutes is up

Air Fryer Chicken Wings

Servings: 4
Cooking Time: 10 Mints

Ingredients:
- 900 g chicken wings
- Salt
- Freshlyground black pepper
- Nonstick cooking spray
- 60 ml hot sauce
- 57 g/4 tbsp. melted butter
- 1 tsp. Worcestershire sauce
- 1/2 tsp. garlic powder
- Blue cheese dressing, for serving

Directions:
1. Season wings all over with salt and pepper, and coat the inside of air fryer with nonstick cooking spray.
2. Set air fryer to 190°C/375°F and cook wings 12 minutes. Remove the air fryer tray, flip wings, and cook 12 minutes more. Increase heat to 200°C/400°F and cook 5 minutes more.
3. Meanwhile, in a large bowl, whisk to combine hot sauce, butter, Worcestershire sauce, and garlic powder. Add cooked wings and toss gently to coat. Serve hot with blue cheese dressing for dipping

Chicken Tikka Masala

Servings: 4

Ingredients:
- 100g tikka masala curry pasta
- 200g low fat yogurt
- 600g skinless chicken breasts
- 1 tbsp vegetable oil
- 1 onion, chopped
- 400g can of the whole, peeled tomatoes
- 20ml water
- 1 tbsp sugar
- 2 tbsp lemon juice
- 1 small bunch of chopped coriander leaves

Directions:
1. Take a bowl and combine the tikka masala curry paste with half the yogurt
2. Cut the chicken into strips
3. Preheat the air fryer to 200ºC
4. Add the yogurt mixture and coat the chicken until fully covered
5. Place into the refrigerator for 2 hours
6. Place the oil and onion in the air fryer and cook for 10 minutes
7. Add the marinated chicken, tomatoes, water and the rest of the yogurt and combine
8. Add the sugar and lemon juice and combine again
9. Cook for 15 minutes

Smoky Chicken Breast

Servings: 2

Ingredients:
- 2 halved chicken breasts
- 2 tsp olive oil
- 1 tsp ground thyme
- 2 tsp paprika
- 1tsp cumin
- 0.5 tsp cayenne pepper
- 0.5 tsp onion powder
- Salt and pepper to taste

Directions:
1. In a medium bowl, combine the spices together
2. Pour the spice mixture onto a plate
3. Take each chicken breast and coat in the spices, pressing down to ensure an even distribution
4. Place the chicken to one side for 5 minutes
5. Preheat your air fryer to 180ºC
6. Arrange the chicken inside the fryer and cook for 10 minutes
7. Turn the chicken over and cook for another 10 minutes
8. Remove from the fryer and allow to sit for 5 minutes before serving

Air Fryer Chicken Strips

Servings: 4
Cooking Time: 15 Mints

Ingredients:
- 454 g chicken tenders , or boneless skinless chicken breast, tenders, or thighs
- 240-480 ml Panko – or breading of choice-breadcrumbs, crushed pork rinds, almond flour, etc
- 2 eggs
- 1 teaspoon salt , or to taste
- 1/2 teaspoon black pepper , or to taste
- 1 teaspoon garlic powder
- 1 teaspoon paprik

Directions:
1. Preheat the Air Fryer at 370°F/188°C for 4 minutes.
2. If not using tenders, cut the chicken into strips. Make sure they are evenly sized. The thicker they are, the longer they will take to cook.
3. Combine the seasonings (salt, pepper, garlic powder and paprika). Season the chicken strips with the spices. Put the Panko (or breading of choice) in a bowl large enough to dredge the chicken. In another bowl, beat the eggs until smooth.
4. Coat the chicken cutlets strips in egg, then in the Panko (or breading of choice). Press chicken strips into the Panko so that it sticks and completely coats the chicken. Repeat for all chicken pieces.
5. Generously spray both sides of all the coated chicken with oil spray to coat all dry spots.
6. Air Fry at 370°F/190°C for 6 minutes. Gently flip the tenders and lightly spray any dry spots. Continue to air fry for another 2-8 minutes (depending on the size and thickness of your tenders), or until they are crispy brown or internal temperature of the chicken reaches 165°F/74°C.

Beef & Lamb And Pork Recipes
Char Siu Buffalo

Servings: 2

Ingredients:
- 1 kg beef, cut into strips
- 4 tbsp honey
- 2 tbsp sugar
- 2 tbsp char siu sauce
- 2 tbsp oyster sauce
- 2 tbsp soy sauce
- 2 tbsp olive oil
- 2 tsp minced garlic
- ¼ tsp bi carbonate of soda

Directions:
1. Place all the ingredients in a bowl, mix well and marinate over night
2. Line the air fryer with foil, add the beef, keep the marinade to one side
3. Cook at 200ºC for 10 minutes
4. Brush the pork with the sauce and cook for another 20 minutes at 160ºC
5. Remove the meat and set aside
6. Strain the marinade into a saucepan, heat until it thickens
7. Drizzle over the pork and serve with rice

Homemade Crispy Pepperoni Pizza

Servings: 4
Cooking Time: 10 Minutes

Ingredients:

- For the pizza dough:
- 500 g / 17.6 oz plain flour
- 1 tsp salt
- 1 tsp dry non-fast-acting yeast
- 400 ml warm water
- For the toppings:
- 100 g / 3.5 oz tomato sauce
- 100 g / 3.5 oz mozzarella cheese, grated
- 8 slices pepperoni

Directions:

1. To make the pizza dough, place the plain flour, salt, and dry yeast in a large mixing bowl. Pour in the warm water bit by bit until it forms a tacky dough.
2. Lightly dust a clean kitchen top surface with plain flour and roll the dough out until it is around ½ an inch thick.
3. Preheat your air fryer to 150 °C / 300 °F and line the bottom of the basket with parchment paper.
4. Spread the tomato sauce evenly across the dough and top with grated mozzarella cheese. Top with the pepperoni slices and carefully transfer the pizza into the lined air fryer basket.
5. Cook the pizza until the crust is golden and crispy, and the mozzarella cheese has melted.
6. Enjoy the pizza while still hot with a side salad and some potato wedges.

Parmesan Crusted Pork Chops

Servings: 6

Ingredients:

- 6 pork chops
- ½ tsp salt
- ¼ tsp pepper
- 1 tsp paprika
- 3 tbsp parmesan
- ½ tsp onion powder
- ¼ tsp chilli powder
- 2 eggs beaten
- 250g pork rind crumbs

Directions:

1. Preheat the air fryer to 200°C
2. Season the pork with the seasonings
3. Place the pork rind into a food processor and blend into crumbs
4. Mix the pork rind and seasonings in a bowl
5. Beat the eggs in a separate bowl
6. Dip the pork into the egg then into the crumb mix
7. Place pork in the air fryer and cook for about 15 minutes until crispy

Air Fryer Roast Pork Belly

Servings: 4
Cooking Time: 55 Mints
Ingredients:
- 1kg piece boneless pork belly, rind scored
- 2 tsp sea salt flakes
- Olive oil spray

Directions:
1. Preheat the air fryer to 200°C/400°F for 3 minutes. Pat pork dry with paper towel. Rub salt into pork rind.
2. Place the pork in the air fryer basket and spray with oil. Set timer for 25 minutes and cook until the rind crackles. Reduce temperature to 160°C/320°F. Set timer for 30 minutes and cook until pork is tender and cooked through

Copycat Burger

Servings: 4
Ingredients:
- 400g minced pork
- 4 wholemeal burger buns
- Avocado sauce to taste
- 1 avocado
- 1 small onion, chopped
- 2 chopped spring onions
- Salad garnish
- 1 tbsp Worcester sauce
- 1 tbsp tomato ketchup
- 1 tsp garlic puree
- 1 tsp mixed herbs

Directions:
1. In a bowl mix together the mince, onion, half the avocado and all of the seasoning
2. Form into burgers
3. Place in the air fryer and cook at 180°C for 8 minutes
4. When cooked place in the bun, layer with sauce and salad garnish

Mediterranean Beef Meatballs

Servings: 3

Ingredients:
- 500 g/1 lb. 2 oz. minced/ground beef
- 30 g/½ cup fresh breadcrumbs (gluten-free if you wish)
- 1 egg
- 1 teaspoon dried thyme
- ¾ teaspoon salt
- ½ teaspoon freshly ground black pepper
- Mediterranean Sauce or 400-g/14-oz. jar tomato-based pasta sauce
- spaghetti, basil leaves and freshly grated Parmesan, to serve

Directions:
1. Combine all the ingredients (not the sauce) together in a bowl, then divide into 9 equal portions and mould into meatballs.
2. Preheat the air-fryer to 180°C/350°F.
3. Place the meatballs in the preheated air-fryer and air-fry for 8 minutes, turning halfway through cooking.
4. Pour the sauce into a baking dish or gratin dish that fits into your air-fryer. After 8 minutes, pop the meatballs into the sauce in the dish and put the whole dish back into the air-fryer. Cook for a further 5 minutes, then check the internal temperature of the meatballs has reached at least 70°C/160°F using a meat thermometer – if not, cook for another few minutes.
5. Serve the meatballs piled on top of spaghetti, garnished with basil leaves and scattered with grated Parmesan.

Air Fryer Pork Bratwurst

Servings: 2

Ingredients:
- 2 pork bratwursts
- 2 hotdog bread rolls
- 2 tbsp tomato sauce

Directions:
1. Preheat the air fryer to 200°C
2. Place the bratwurst in the fryer and cook for 10 minutes, turning halfway
3. Remove and place in the open bread rolls
4. Place back into the air fryer for 1 to 2 minutes, until the read is slightly crisped
5. Enjoy with the tomato sauce either on top or on the side

Butter Steak & Asparagus

Servings: 6

Ingredients:
- 500g steak, cut into 6 pieces
- Salt and pepper
- 75g tamari sauce
- 2 cloves crushed garlic
- 400g asparagus
- 3 sliced peppers
- 25g balsamic vinegar
- 50g beef broth
- 2 tbsp butter

Directions:
1. Season steaks with salt and pepper
2. Place steaks in a bowl, add tamari sauce and garlic make sure steaks are covered, leave to marinate for at least 1hr
3. Place steaks on a board, fill with peppers and asparagus, roll the steak around and secure with tooth picks
4. Set your fryer to 200ºC and cook for 5 minutes.
5. Whilst cooking heat the broth, butter and balsamic vinegar in a saucepan until thickened
6. Pour over the steaks and serve

Hamburgers

Servings: 4

Ingredients:
- 500g minced beef
- 1 grated onion
- Salt and pepper to taste

Directions:
1. Preheat air fryer to 200ºC
2. Place the grated onion and the beef into a bowl and combine together well
3. Divide minced beef into 4 equal portions, form into patties
4. Season with salt and pepper
5. Place in the air fryer and cook for 10 minutes, turnover and cook for a further 3 minutes

Salt And Pepper Belly Pork

Servings: 4

Ingredients:
- 500g belly pork
- 1 tsp pepper
- ½ tsp salt

Directions:
1. Cut the pork into bite size pieces and season with salt and pepper
2. Heat the air fryer to 200°C
3. Place in the air fryer and cook for 15 minutes until crisp

Tender Ham Steaks

Servings: 1

Ingredients:
- 1 ham steak
- 2 tbsp brown sugar
- 1 tsp honey
- 2 tbsp melted butter

Directions:
1. Preheat the air fryer to 220°C
2. Combine the melted butter and brown sugar until smooth
3. Add the ham to the air fryer and brush both sides with the butter mixture
4. Cook for 12 minutes, turning halfway through and re-brushing the ham
5. Drizzle honey on top before serving

Pork Chilli Cheese Dogs

Servings: 2

Ingredients:

- 1 can of pork chilli, or chilli you have left over
- 200g grated cheese
- 2 hot dog bread rolls
- 2 hot dogs

Directions:

1. Preheat the air fryer to 260°C
2. Cook the hot dogs for 4 minutes, turning halfway
3. Place the hotdogs inside the bread rolls and place back inside the air fryer
4. Top with half the cheese on top and then the chilli
5. Add the rest of the cheese
6. Cook for an extra 2 minutes

Beef Nacho Pinwheels

Servings: 6

Ingredients:

- 500g minced beef
- 1 packet of taco seasoning
- 300ml water
- 300ml sour cream
- 6 tostadas
- 6 flour tortillas
- 3 tomatoes
- 250g nacho cheese
- 250g shredded lettuce
- 250g Mexican cheese

Directions:

1. Preheat air fryer to 200°C
2. Brown the mince in a pan and add the taco seasoning
3. Share the remaining ingredients between the tortillas
4. Fold the edges of the tortillas up towards the centre, should look like a pinwheel
5. Lay seam down in the air fryer and cook for 2 minutes
6. Turnover and cook for a further 2 minutes

Vegetable & Beef Frittata

Servings: 2

Ingredients:
- 250g ground beef
- 4 shredded hash browns
- 8 eggs
- Half a diced onion
- 1 courgette, diced
- 250g grated cheese
- Salt and pepper for seasoning

Directions:
1. Break the ground beef up and place in the air fryer
2. Add the onion and combine well
3. Cook at 260°C for 3 minutes
4. Stir the mixture and cook foremother 2 minutes
5. Remove and clean the tray
6. Add the courgette to the air fryer and spray with a little cooking oil
7. Cook for 3 minutes
8. Add to the meat mixture and combine
9. Take a mixing bowl and combine the cheese, has browns, and eggs
10. Add the meat and courgette to the bowl and season with salt and pepper
11. Take a 6" round baking tray and add the mixture
12. Cook for 8 minutes before cutting lines in the top and cooking for another 8 minutes
13. Cut into slices before serving

Cheesy Meatball Sub

Servings: 2

Ingredients:
- 8 frozen pork meatballs
- 5 tbsp marinara sauce
- 160g grated parmesan cheese
- 2 sub rolls or hotdog rolls
- 1/4 tsp dried oregano

Directions:
1. Preheat the air fryer to 220°C
2. Place the meatball in the air fryer and cook for around 10 minutes, turning halfway through
3. Place the marinara sauce in a bowl
4. Add the meatballs to the sauce and coat completely
5. Add the oregano on top and coat once more
6. Take the bread roll and add the mixture inside
7. Top with the cheese
8. Place the meatball sub back in the air fryer and cook for 2 minutes until the bad is toasted and the cheese has melted

Mustard Pork Tenderloin

Servings: 2

Ingredients:
- 1 pork tenderloin
- 3 tbsp soy sauce
- 2 minced garlic cloves
- 3 tbsp olive oil
- 2 tbsp brown sugar
- 1 tbsp dijon mustard
- Salt and pepper for seasoning

Directions:
1. Take a bowl and combine the ingredients, except for the pork
2. Pour the mixture into a ziplock bag and then add the pork
3. Close the top and make sure the pork is well covered
4. Place in the refrigerator for 30minutes
5. Preheat your air fryer to 260ºC
6. Remove the pork from the bag and place in the fryer
7. Cook for 25 minutes, turning halfway
8. Remove and rest for 5 minutes before slicing into pieces

Japanese Pork Chops

Servings: 4

Ingredients:
- 6 boneless pork chops
- 30g flour
- 2 beaten eggs
- 2 tbsp sweet chilli sauce
- 500g cup seasoned breadcrumbs
- ⅛ tsp salt
- ⅛ tsp pepper
- Tonkatsu sauce to taste

Directions:
1. Place the flour, breadcrumbs and eggs in 3 separate bowls
2. Sprinkle both sides of the pork with salt and pepper
3. Coat the pork in flour, egg and then breadcrumbs
4. Place in the air fryer and cook at 180ºC for 8 minutes, turn then cook for a further 5 minutes
5. Serve with sauces on the side

Beef Wellington

Servings: 4

Ingredients:
- 300g chicken liver pate
- 500g shortcrust pastry
- 600g beef fillet
- 1 egg beaten
- Salt and pepper

Directions:
1. Remove all the visible fat from the beef season with salt and pepper. Wrap in cling film and place in the fridge for 1 hour
2. Roll out the pastry, brush the edges with egg
3. Spread the pate over the pastry. Remove the clingfilm from the beef and place in the center of the pastry
4. Seal the pastry around the meat
5. Place in the air fryer and cook at 160°C for 35 minutes

Chinese Chilli Beef

Servings: 2

Ingredients:
- 4 tbsp light soy sauce
- 1 tsp honey
- 3 tbsp tomato ketchup
- 1 tsp Chinese 5 spice
- 1 tbsp oil
- 6 tbsp sweet chilli sauce
- 1 tbsp lemon juice
- 400g frying steak
- 2 tbsp cornflour

Directions:
1. Slice the steak into strips, put into a bowl and cover with cornflour and 5 spice
2. Add to the air fryer and cook for 6 minutes at 200°C
3. Whilst the beef is cooking mix together the remaining ingredients
4. Add to the air fryer and cook for another 3 minutes

Honey & Mustard Meatballs

Servings: 4

Ingredients:
- 500g minced pork
- 1 red onion
- 1 tsp mustard
- 2 tsp honey
- 1 tsp garlic puree
- 1 tsp pork seasoning
- Salt and pepper

Directions:
1. Thinly slice the onion
2. Place all the ingredients in a bowl and mix until well combined
3. Form into meatballs, place in the air fryer and cook at 180°C for 10 minutes

Air Fryer Breaded Pork Chops

Servings: 3
Cooking Time: 16 Mints

Ingredients:
- 3 (6oz.) (3 (170g)) pork chops, rinsed & patted dry
- salt, to taste
- black pepper, to taste
- garlic powder, to taste
- smoked paprika, to taste
- 1/2 cup (54 g) breadcrumbs, approximately
- 1 large (1 large) egg
- Cooking spray, for coating the pork chops

Directions:
1. Add seasonings to both sides of the pork chops with salt, pepper, garlic powder, and smoked paprika.
2. Add the breadcrumbs in a medium bowl. In another bowl, beat the egg.
3. Dip each pork chop in egg and then dredge it in the breadcrumbs, coating completely. Lightly spray both sides of coated pork chops with cooking spray right before cooking.
4. Preheat the Air Fryer at 380°F/193°C for 4 minutes. This will give the pork chops a nice crunchy crust.
5. Place in the Air Fryer and cook at 380°F/193°C for 8-12 minutes. After 6 minutes of cooking, flip the pork chops and then continue cooking for the remainder of time or until golden and internal temperature reaches 145-160°F/60-70°C
6. Serve warm.

Pork Taquitos

Servings: 5

Ingredients:
- 400g shredded pork
- 500g grated mozzarella
- 10 flour tortillas
- The juice of 1 lime
- Cooking spray

Directions:
1. Preheat air fryer to 190ºC
2. Sprinkle lime juice on the pork and mix
3. Microwave tortilla for about 10 seconds to soften
4. Add a little pork and cheese to a tortilla
5. Roll then tortilla up, and place in the air fryer
6. Cook for about 7 minutes until golden, turn halfway through cooking

Fish & Seafood Recipes
Peppery Lemon Shrimp

Servings: 2

Ingredients:
- 300g uncooked shrimp
- 1 tbsp olive oil
- 1 the juice of 1 lemon
- 0.25 tsp garlic powder
- 1 sliced lemon
- 1 tsp pepper
- 0.25 tsp paprika

Directions:
1. Heat the fryer to 200ºC
2. Take a medium sized mixing bowl and combine the lemon juice, pepper, garlic powder, paprika and the olive oil together
3. Add the shrimp to the bowl and make sure they're well coated
4. Arrange the shrimp into the basket of the fryer
5. Cook for between 6-8 minutes, until firm and pink

Tilapia Fillets

Servings: 2

Ingredients:
- 2 tbsp melted butter
- 150g almond flour
- 3 tbsp mayonnaise
- 2 tilapia fillets
- 25g thinly sliced almonds
- Salt and pepper to taste
- Vegetable oil spray

Directions:
1. Mix the almond flour, butter, pepper and salt together in a bowl
2. Spread mayonnaise on both sides of the fish
3. Cover the fillets in the almond flour mix
4. Spread one side of the fish with the sliced almonds
5. Spray the air fryer with the vegetable spray
6. Place in the air fryer and cook at 160°C for 10 minutes

Chilli Lime Tilapia

Servings: 3

Ingredients:
- 500g Tilapia fillets
- 25g panko crumbs
- 200g flour
- Salt and pepper to taste
- 2 eggs
- 1 tbsp chilli powder
- The juice of 1 lime

Directions:
1. Mix panko, salt and pepper and chilli powder together
2. Whisk the egg in a separate bowl
3. Spray the air fryer with cooking spray
4. Dip the tilapia in the flour, then in the egg and cover in the panko mix
5. Place fish in the air fryer, spray with cooking spray and cook for 7-8 minutes at 190°C
6. Turn the fish over and cook for a further 7-8 minutes until golden brown.
7. Squeeze lime juice over the top and serve

Copycat Fish Fingers

Servings: 2

Ingredients:

- 2 slices wholemeal bread, grated into breadcrumbs
- 50g plain flour
- 1 beaten egg
- 1 white fish fillet
- The juice of 1 small lemon
- 1 tsp parsley
- 1 tsp thyme
- 1 tsp mixed herbs
- Salt and pepper to taste

Directions:
1. Preheat the air fryer to 180°C
2. Add salt pepper and parsley to the breadcrumbs and combine well
3. Place the egg in another bowl
4. Place the flour in a separate bowl
5. Place the fish into a food processor and add the lemon juice, salt, pepper thyme and mixed herbs
6. Blitz to create a crumb-like consistency
7. Roll your fish in the flour, then the egg and then the breadcrumbs
8. Cook at 180°C for 8 minutes

Crispy Cajun Fish Fingers

Servings: 2

Ingredients:

- 350 g/12 oz. cod loins
- 1 teaspoon smoked paprika
- ½ teaspoon cayenne pepper
- ½ teaspoon onion granules
- ¾ teaspoon dried oregano
- ¼ teaspoon dried thyme
- ½ teaspoon salt
- ½ teaspoon unrefined sugar
- 40 g/½ cup dried breadcrumbs (gluten-free if you wish, see page 9)
- 2 tablespoons plain/all-purpose flour (gluten-free if you wish)
- 1 egg, beaten

Directions:
1. Slice the cod into 6 equal fish 'fingers'. Mix the spices, herbs, salt and sugar together, then combine with the breadcrumbs. Lay out three bowls: one with flour, one with beaten egg and one with the Cajun-spiced breadcrumbs. Dip each fish finger into the flour, then the egg, then the breadcrumbs until fully coated.
2. Preheat the air-fryer to 180°C/350°F.
3. Add the fish to the preheated air-fryer and air-fry for 6 minutes, until cooked inside. Check the internal temperature of the fish has reached at least 75°C/167°F using a meat thermometer – if not, cook for another few minutes.

Air Fryer Tuna Mornay Parcels

Servings: 2-3
Cooking Time: 30 Mints

Ingredients:

- 30 g butter
- 2 green shallots, thickly sliced
- 2 tbsp plain flour
- 310ml /1 1/4 cups milk
- 80 g/1 cup coarsely grated cheddar
- 185 g can tuna in oil, drained, flaked
- 120 g /3/4 cup frozen mixed vegetables (peas and corn)
- 2 sheets frozen puff pastry, just thawed
- 1 egg, lightly whisked

Directions:

1. Heat the butter in a medium saucepan over medium heat until melted. Add the shallot and cook, stirring, for 2 minutes or until soft. Add the flour and cook, stirring, for 1 minute. Gradually add the milk, stirring constantly, until smooth. Bring to a simmer. Cook, stirring, for 2 minutes or until thickened slightly. Remove from heat and stir in the cheese . Transfer to a large bowl. Set aside to cool until room temperature.
2. Add the tuna and frozen veg to the white sauce and stir until just combined. Cut each pastry sheet into 4 squares. Place 1/4 cupful tuna mixture into the centre of each square. Fold corners of pastry towards the centre to enclose the filling. Pinch to seal.
3. Preheat air fryer to 190°C/320°F for 2 minutes. Brush parcels with egg. Grease the base of air fryer basket with oil. Place 4 parcels into the basket and cook for 8 minutes or until light golden. Turn and cook for a further 3 minutes or until golden. Repeat with remaining parcels. Serve.

Air Fryer Spicy Bay Scallops

Servings: 4
Cooking Time: 10 Mints

Ingredients:

- 454 g bay scallops, rinsed and patted dry
- 2 teaspoons smoked paprika
- 2 teaspoons chili powder
- 2 teaspoons olive oil
- 1 teaspoon garlic powder
- ¼ teaspoon ground black pepper
- ⅛ teaspoon cayenne red pepper

Directions:

1. Preheat an air fryer to 400°F/200°C.
2. Combine bay scallops, smoked paprika, chili powder, olive oil, garlic powder, pepper, and cayenne pepper in a bowl; stir until evenly combined. Transfer to the air fryer basket.
3. Air fry until scallops are cooked through, about 8 minutes, shaking basket halfway through the cooking time.

Garlic Butter Salmon

Servings: 2

Ingredients:

- 2 salmon fillets, boneless with the skin left on
- 1 tsp minced garlic
- 2 tbsp melted butter
- 1 tsp chopped parsley
- Salt and pepper to taste

Directions:

1. Preheat the air fryer to 270 ºC
2. Take a bowl and combine the melted butter, parsley and garlic to create a sauce
3. Season the salmon to your liking
4. Brush the salmon with the garlic mixture, on both sides
5. Place the salmon into the fryer, with the skin side facing down
6. Cook for 10 minutes - the salmon is done when it flakes with ease

Salt & Pepper Calamari

Servings: 2

Ingredients:

- 500g squid rings
- 500g panko breadcrumbs
- 250g plain flour
- 2 tbsp pepper
- 2 tbsp salt
- 200ml buttermilk
- 1 egg

Directions:

1. Take a medium bowl and combine the buttermilk and egg, stirring well
2. Take another bowl and combine the salt, pepper, flour, and panko breadcrumbs, combining again
3. Dip the quid into the buttermilk first and then the breadcrumbs, coating evenly
4. Place in the air fryer basket
5. Cook at 150ºC for 12 minutes, until golden

Sea Bass With Asparagus Spears

Servings: 2

Ingredients:
- 2 x 100-g/3½-oz. sea bass fillets
- 8 asparagus spears
- 2 teaspoons olive oil
- salt and freshly ground black pepper
- boiled new potatoes, to serve
- CAPER DRESSING
- 1½ tablespoons olive oil
- grated zest and freshly squeezed juice of ½ lemon
- 1 tablespoon small, jarred capers
- 1 teaspoon Dijon mustard
- 1 tablespoon freshly chopped flat-leaf parsley

Directions:
1. Preheat the air-fryer to 180ºC/350ºF.
2. Prepare the fish and asparagus by brushing both with the olive oil and sprinkling over salt and pepper.
3. Add the asparagus to the preheated air-fryer and air-fry for 4 minutes, then turn the asparagus and add the fish to the air-fryer drawer. Cook for a further 4 minutes. Check the internal temperature of the fish has reached at least 60ºC/140ºF using a meat thermometer – if not, cook for another minute.
4. Meanwhile, make the dressing by combining all the ingredients in a jar and shaking well. Pour the dressing over the cooked fish and asparagus spears and serve with new potatoes.

Salmon Patties

Servings: 4

Ingredients:
- 400g salmon
- 1 egg
- 1 diced onion
- 200g breadcrumbs
- 1 tsp dill weed

Directions:
1. Remove all bones and skin from the salmon
2. Mix egg, onion, dill weed and bread crumbs with the salmon
3. Shape mixture into patties and place into the air fryer
4. Set air fryer to 180ºC
5. Cook for 5 minutes then turn them over and cook for a further 5 minutes until golden brown

Alba Salad With Air Fried Butterfly Shrimp

Servings: 2
Cooking Time: 6 Mints
Ingredients:
- 250 g Butterfly Shrimp
- 5 cups arugula
- 12 g/½ cup Kalamata olives, pitted
- 56 g/2 oz Roquefort, crumbled
- 1 pear
- 1 avocado
- 2 celery stalks
- 112 g/4 oz canned mushrooms, drained
- For the dressing:
- 3 tbsp olive oil
- 1 small garlic clove
- 1 tbsp freshly squeezed lemon juice or apple cider vinegar
- 1 tsp Dijon mustard
- ½ tsp kosher sea salt
- ¼ tsp freshly-cracked black pepper

Directions:
1. Place Gorton's Butterfly Shrimp on air fryer rack and air fry at 200°C/400°F for 11 – 13 minutes, until reaching an internal temperature of 145°C/300°F or higher.
2. Chop pear, avocado, and celery stalk into bite-sized pieces.
3. Add arugula, Calamata olives, crumbled Roquefort, drained mushrooms, chopped pear, and avocado to a medium bowl.
4. For the dressing, finely chop garlic clove. Add all ingredients in a small bowl and mix with a fork or whisk.
5. Gently mix in the Alba Salad Dressing. Add the salad to a medium serving platter. Top with the air fried Butterfly Shrimp. Enjoy!

Extra Crispy Popcorn Shrimp

Servings: 2
Ingredients:
- 300g Frozen popcorn shrimp
- 1 tsp cayenne pepper
- Salt and pepper for seasoning

Directions:
1. Preheat the air fryer to 220°C
2. Place the shrimp inside the air fryer and cook for 6 minutes, giving them a shake at the halfway point
3. Remove and season with salt and pepper, and the cayenne to your liking

Air Fryer Lemon Pepper Shrimp

Servings: 2
Cooking Time: 15 Mints
Ingredients:
- 1 tablespoon olive oil
- 1 lemon, juiced
- 1 teaspoon lemon pepper
- ¼ teaspoon paprika
- ¼ teaspoon garlic powder
- 340 g uncooked medium shrimp, peeled and deveined
- 1 lemon, sliced

Directions:
1. Preheat an air fryer to 400°F 200°C according to the manufacturer's instructions.
2. Combine oil, lemon juice, lemon pepper, paprika, and garlic powder in a bowl. Add shrimp and toss to coat.
3. Cook shrimp in the preheated air fryer until they are bright pink on the outside and the meat is opaque, about 6 to 8 minutes. Serve with lemon slices.

Tandoori Salmon

Servings: 4
Ingredients:
- 300g salmon
- 1 tbsp butter
- 1 tbsp tandoori spice
- Salt and pepper to taste
- 1 small tomato
- Half a red onion
- 600g plain yogurt
- 30 fresh mint leaves, chopped
- 1 tsp minced green chilli
- 1 tbsp ground cumin
- Half a cucumber, chopped

Directions:
1. Cut the salmon into cubes and coat in the tandoori spice mix. Chill for 30 minutes to marinate
2. Blend mint, cumin and chilli with ¼ of the yogurt refrigerate and leave to steep
3. Peel the tomato and cut into cubes. Peel the cucumber and chop into cubes, finely dice the onion
4. Cook the salmon in the air fryer for 5-6 minutes at 200°C
5. Mix the flavoured yogurt with the remaining yogurt, tomato, cucumber and onion
6. Place the sauce in serving bowls and place the salmon on top

Store-cupboard Fishcakes

Servings: 3

Ingredients:
- 400 g/14 oz. cooked potato – either mashed potato or the insides of jacket potatoes (see page 124)
- 2 x 150–200-g/5½–7-oz. cans fish, such as tuna or salmon, drained
- 2 eggs
- ¾ teaspoon salt
- 1 teaspoon dried parsley
- ½ teaspoon freshly ground black pepper
- 1 tablespoon olive oil
- caper dressing (see page 79), to serve

Directions:
1. Mix the cooked potato, fish, eggs, salt, parsley and pepper together in a bowl, then divide into 6 equal portions and form into fishcakes. Drizzle the olive oil over both sides of each fishcake.
2. Preheat the air-fryer to 180°C/350°F.
3. Add the fishcakes to the preheated air-fryer and air-fry for 15 minutes, turning halfway through cooking. Serve with salad and tartare sauce or Caper Dressing.

Air Fryer Salmon Fillets

Servings: 2
Cooking Time: 5 Mints

Ingredients:
- 1 slice day-old bread
- 25 g butter, melted
- 2 tsp chopped fresh dill, plus extra, to serve
- 2 tsp chopped fresh chives
- 2 (about 180g each) skinless salmon fillets
- Extra virgin olive oil, to serve
- Lemon wedges, to serve

Directions:
1. Place the bread in a small food processor. Process until fine crumbs form. Transfer to a bowl. Add butter , dill and chives to the bowl. Season. Stir well to combine. Press mixture over the top of each salmon fillet.
2. Place the herb-crusted salmon in the basket. Cook for 4 minutes at 180°C/350°F or until salmon is cooked to your liking. Drizzle with oil. Serve with lemon wedges and fresh dill.

Honey Sriracha Salmon

Servings: 2

Ingredients:

- 25g sriracha
- 25g honey
- 500g salmon fillets
- 1 tbsp soy sauce

Directions:

1. Mix the honey, soy sauce and sriracha, keep half the mix to one side for dipping
2. Place the salmon in the sauce skin side up and marinade for 30 minutes
3. Spray air fryer basket with cooking spray
4. Heat the air fryer to 200ºC
5. Place salmon in the air fryer skin side down and cook for 12 minutes

Air Fried Fish Tostadas With Mango Salsa

Servings: 4
Cooking Time: 10 Mints

Ingredients:

- 4 tostada shells
- 8 Gorton's Beer Battered Fish Tenders
- 160 g fresh mango, diced
- 1 small jalapeno (about 2 Tablespoons), diced
- 1 Tablespoon fresh cilantro, minced
- 1 lime, juiced
- 1-2 Tablespoons red onion, minced salt to taste

Directions:

1. Cook your Gorton's Beer Battered Fish Tenders in the air fryer at 200°C/400°F for 9 – 10 minutes, until reaching an internal temperature of 165°C/320°F or higher.
2. While the Gorton's Seafood Beer Battered Fish Tenders are in the air fryer, prepare your mango salsa. Add mango, jalapeno, cilantro, lime, and red onion to a small bowl and mix until combined.
3. Place two Gorton's Seafood Beer Battered Fish Tenders on a single tostada shell then top with a healthy scoop of your fresh mango salsa. Enjoy!

Cajun Shrimp Boil

Servings: 6

Ingredients:
- 300g cooked shrimp
- 14 slices of smoked sausage
- 5 par boiled potatoes, cut into halves
- 4 mini corn on the cobs, quartered
- 1 diced onion
- 3 tbsp old bay seasoning
- Olive oil spray

Directions:
1. Combine all the ingredients in a bowl and mix well
2. Line the air fryer with foil
3. Place half the mix into the air fryer and cook at 200°C for about 6 minutes, mix the ingredients and cook for a further 6 minutes.
4. Repeat for the second batch

Air Fryer Tuna

Servings: 2

Ingredients:
- 2 tuna steaks, boneless and skinless
- 2 tsp honey
- 1 tsp grated ginger
- 4 tbsp soy sauce
- 1 tsp sesame oil
- 1/2 tsp rice vinegar

Directions:
1. Combine the honey, soy sauce, rice vinegar and sesame oil in a bowl until totally mixed together
2. Cover the tuna steaks with the sauce and place in the refrigerator for half an hour to marinade
3. Preheat the air fryer to 270°C
4. Cook the tuna for 4 minutes
5. Allow to rest before slicing

Cajun Prawn Skewers

Servings: 2

Ingredients:
- 350 g/12 oz. king prawns/jumbo shrimp
- MARINADE
- 1 teaspoon smoked paprika
- 1 teaspoon unrefined sugar
- 1 teaspoon salt
- ½ teaspoon onion powder
- ½ teaspoon mustard powder
- ¼ teaspoon dried oregano
- ¼ teaspoon dried thyme
- 1 teaspoon white wine vinegar
- 2 teaspoons olive oil

Directions:
1. Mix all the marinade ingredients together in a bowl. Mix the prawns/shrimp into the marinade and cover. Place in the fridge to marinate for at least an hour.
2. Preheat the air-fryer to 180ºC/350ºF.
3. Thread 4–5 prawns/shrimp on to each skewer (you should have enough for 4–5 skewers). Add the skewers to the preheated air-fryer and air-fry for 2 minutes, then turn the skewers and cook for a further 2 minutes. Check the internal temperature of the prawns/shrimp has reached at least 50ºC/125ºF using a meat thermometer – if not, cook for another few minutes. Serve immediately.

Side Dishes Recipes

Garlic And Parsley Potatoes

Servings: 4

Ingredients:
- 500g baby potatoes, cut into quarters
- 1 tbsp oil
- 1 tsp salt
- ½ tsp garlic powder
- ½ tsp dried parsley

Directions:
1. Preheat air fryer to 175ºC
2. Combine potatoes and oil in a bowl
3. Add remaining ingredients and mix
4. Add to the air fryer and cook for about 25 minutes until golden brown, turning halfway through

Sweet Potato Tots

Servings: 24

Ingredients:
- 2 sweet potatoes, peeled
- ½ tsp cajun seasoning
- Olive oil cooking spray
- Sea salt to taste

Directions:
1. Boil the sweet potatoes in a pan for about 15 minutes, allow to cool
2. Grate the sweet potato and mix in the cajun seasoning
3. Form into tot shaped cylinders
4. Spray the air fryer with oil, place the tots in the air fryer
5. Sprinkle with salt and cook for 8 minutes at 200°C, turn and cook for another 8 minutes

Zingy Roasted Carrots

Servings: 4

Ingredients:
- 500g carrots
- 1 tsp olive oil
- 1 tsp cayenne pepper
- Salt and pepper for seasoning

Directions:
1. Peel the carrots and cut them into chunks, around 2" in size
2. Preheat your air fryer to 220°C
3. Add the carrots to a bowl with the olive oil and cayenne and toss to coat
4. Place in the fryer and cook for 15 minutes, giving them a stir halfway through
5. Season before serving

Grilled Bacon And Cheese

Servings: 2

Ingredients:
- 4 slices of regular bread
- 1 tbsp butter
- 2 slices cheddar cheese
- 5 slices bacon, pre-cooked
- 2 slices mozzarella cheese

Directions:
1. Place the butter into the microwave to melt
2. Spread the butter onto one side of the bread slices
3. Place one slice of bread into the fryer basket, with the buttered side facing downwards
4. Place the cheddar on top, followed by the bacon, mozzarella and the other slice of bread, with the buttered side facing upwards
5. Set your fryer to 170°C and cook the sandwich for 4 minutes
6. Turn the sandwich over and cook for another 3 minutes
7. Turn the sandwich out and serve whilst hot
8. Repeat with the other remaining sandwich

Potato Wedges

Servings: 4

Ingredients:
- 2 potatoes, cut into wedges
- 1 ½ tbsp olive oil
- ½ tsp paprika
- ⅛ tsp ground black pepper
- ½ tsp parsley flakes
- ½ tsp chilli powder
- ½ tsp sea salt

Directions:
1. Preheat the air fryer to 200°C
2. Add all ingredients to a bowl and combine well
3. Place the wedges into the air fryer and cook for 10 minutes
4. Turn and cook for a further 8 minutes until golden brown

Orange Sesame Cauliflower

Servings: 4

Ingredients:
- 100ml water
- 30g cornstarch
- 50g flour
- 1/2 tsp salt
- ½ tsp pepper
- 2 tbsp tomato ketchup
- 2 tbsp brown sugar
- 1 sliced onion

Directions:
1. Mix together flour, cornstarch, water, salt and pepper until smooth
2. Coat the cauliflower and chill for 30 minutes
3. Place in the air fryer and cook for 22 minutes at 170ºC
4. Meanwhile combine remaining ingredients in a saucepan, gently simmer until thickened.
5. Mix cauliflower with sauce and top with toasted sesame seeds to serve

Bbq Beetroot Crisps

Servings:4
Cooking Time:5 Minutes

Ingredients:
- 400 g / 14 oz beetroot, sliced
- 2 tbsp olive oil
- 1 tbsp BBQ seasoning
- ½ tsp black pepper

Directions:
1. Preheat the air fryer to 180 °C / 350 °F and line the bottom of the basket with parchment paper.
2. Place the beetroot slices in a large bowl. Add the olive oil, BBQ seasoning, and black pepper, and toss to coat the beetroot slices on both sides.
3. Place the beetroot slices in the air fryer and cook for 5 minutes until hot and crispy.

Stuffed Jacket Potatoes

Servings: 4

Ingredients:

- 2 large russet potatoes
- 2 tsp olive oil
- 100ml yoghurt
- 100ml milk
- ¼ tsp pepper
- 50g chopped spinach
- 2 tbsp nutritional yeast
- ½ tsp salt

Directions:

1. Preheat the air fryer to 190°C
2. Rub the potatoes with oil
3. Place the potatoes in the air fryer and cook for 30 minutes, turn and cook for a further 30 minutes
4. Cut each potato in half and scoop out the middles, mash with yoghurt, milk and yeast. Stir in the spinach and season with salt and pepper
5. Add the mix back into the potato skins and place in the air fryer, cook at 160°C for about 5 mins

Egg Fried Rice

Servings: 2

Cooking Time: 15 Minutes

Ingredients:

- 400 g / 14 oz cooked white or brown rice
- 100 g / 3.5 oz fresh peas and sweetcorn
- 2 tbsp olive oil
- 2 eggs, scrambled

Directions:

1. Preheat the air fryer to 150 °C / 300 °F and line the bottom of the basket with parchment paper.
2. In a bowl, mix the cooked white or brown rice and the fresh peas and sweetcorn.
3. Pour in 2 tbsp olive oil and toss to coat evenly. Stir in the scrambled eggs.
4. Transfer the egg rice into the lined air fryer basket, close the lid, and cook for 15 minutes until the eggs are cooked and the rice is soft.
5. Serve as a side dish with some cooked meat or tofu.

Shishito Peppers

Servings: 2

Ingredients:
- 200g shishito peppers
- Salt and pepper to taste
- ½ tbsp avocado oil
- 75g grated cheese
- 2 limes

Directions:
1. Rinse the peppers
2. Place in a bowl and mix with oil, salt and pepper
3. Place in the air fryer and cook at 175°C for 10 minutes
4. Place on a serving plate and sprinkle with cheese

Potato Wedges With Rosemary

Servings: 2

Ingredients:
- 2 potatoes, sliced into wedges
- 1 tbsp olive oil
- 2 tsp seasoned salt
- 2 tbsp chopped rosemary

Directions:
1. Preheat air fryer to 190°C
2. Drizzle potatoes with oil, mix in salt and rosemary
3. Place in the air fryer and cook for 20 minutes turning halfway

Air Fryer Eggy Bread

Servings: 2
Cooking Time: 5-7 Minutes

Ingredients:
- 4 slices white bread
- 4 eggs, beaten
- 1 tsp black pepper
- 1 tsp dried chives

Directions:
1. Preheat your air fryer to 150 °C / 300 °F and line the bottom of the basket with parchment paper.
2. Whisk the eggs in a large mixing bowl and soak each slice of bread until fully coated.
3. Transfer the eggy bread to the preheated air fryer and cook for 5-7 minutes until the eggs are set and the bread is crispy.
4. Serve hot with a sprinkle of black pepper and chives on top.

Crispy Cinnamon French Toast

Servings: 2
Cooking Time: 5 Minutes

Ingredients:
- 4 slices white bread
- 4 eggs
- 200 ml milk (cow's milk, cashew milk, soy milk, or oat milk)
- 2 tbsp granulated sugar
- 1 tsp brown sugar
- 1 tsp vanilla extract
- ½ tsp ground cinnamon

Directions:
1. Preheat your air fryer to 150 °C / 300 °F and line the bottom of the basket with parchment paper.
2. Cut each of the bread slices into 2 even rectangles and set them aside.
3. In a mixing bowl, whisk together the 4 eggs, milk, granulated sugar, brown sugar, vanilla extract, and ground cinnamon.
4. Soak the bread pieces in the egg mixture until they are fully covered and soaked in the mixture.
5. Place the coated bread slices in the lined air fryer, close the lid, and cook for 4-5 minutes until the bread is crispy and golden.
6. Serve the French toast slices with whatever toppings you desire.

Mexican Rice

Servings: 4

Ingredients:
- 500g long grain rice
- 3 tbsp olive oil
- 60ml water
- 1 tsp chilli powder
- 1/4 tsp cumin
- 2 tbsp tomato paste
- 1/2 tsp garlic powder
- 1tsp red pepper flakes
- 1 chopped onion
- 500ml chicken stock
- Half a small jalapeño pepper with seeds out, chopped
- Salt for seasoning

Directions:
1. Add the water and tomato paste and combine, placing to one side
2. Take a baking pan and add a little oil
3. Wash the rice and add to the baking pan
4. Add the chicken stock, tomato paste, jalapeños, onions, and the rest of the olive oil, and combine
5. Place aluminium foil over the top and place in your air fryer
6. Cook at 220°C for 50 minutes
7. Keep checking the rice as it cooks, as the liquid should be absorbing

Air Fryer Corn On The Cob

Servings: 2

Ingredients:
- 2 corn on the cob
- 2 tbsp melted butter
- A pinch of salt
- 1/2 tsp dried parsley
- 2 tbsp grated parmesan

Directions:
1. Preheat the air fryer to 270°C
2. Take a bowl and combine the melted butter, salt and parsley
3. Brush the corn with the mixture
4. Add the corn inside the air fryer and cook for 14 minutes
5. Remove the corn from the fryer and roll in the grated cheese

Roasted Okra

Servings: 1

Ingredients:

- 300g Okra, ends trimmed and pods sliced
- 1 tsp olive oil
- ¼ tsp salt
- ⅛ tsp pepper

Directions:

1. Preheat the air fryer to 175°C
2. Combine all ingredients in a bowl and stir gently
3. Place in the air fryer and cook for 5 minutes, shake and cook for another 5 minutes

Pumpkin Fries

Servings: 4

Ingredients:

- 1 small pumpkin, seeds removed and peeled, cut into half inch slices
- 2 tsp olive oil
- 1 tsp garlic powder
- 1/2 tsp paprika
- A pinch of salt

Directions:

1. Take a large bowl and add the slices of pumpkin
2. Add the oil and all the seasonings. Toss to coat well
3. Place in the air fryer
4. Cook at 280°C for 15 minutes, until the chips are tender, shaking at the halfway point

Courgette Gratin

Servings: 2

Ingredients:
- 2 courgette
- 1 tbsp chopped parsley
- 2 tbsp breadcrumbs
- 4 tbsp grated parmesan
- 1 tbsp vegetable oil
- Salt and pepper to taste

Directions:
1. Heat the air fryer to 180°C
2. Cut each courgette in half length ways then slice
3. Mix the remaining ingredients together
4. Place the courgette in the air fryer and top with the breadcrumb mix
5. Cook for about 15 minutes until golden brown

Vegetarian & Vegan Recipes

Radish Hash Browns

Servings: 4

Ingredients:
- 300g radish
- 1 onion
- 1 tsp onion powder
- ¾ tsp sea salt
- ½ tsp paprika
- ¼ tsp ground black pepper
- 1 tsp coconut oil

Directions:
1. Wash the radish, trim off the roots and slice in a processor along with the onions
2. Add the coconut oil and mix well
3. Put the onions and radish into the air fryer and cook at 180°C for 8 minutes shaking a few times
4. Put the onion and radish in a bowl add seasoning and mix well
5. Put back in the air fryer and cook at 200°C for 5 minutes

Crispy Sweet & Spicy Cauliflower

Servings: 2

Ingredients:
- ½ a head of cauliflower
- 1 teaspoon sriracha sauce
- 1 teaspoon soy sauce (or tamari)
- ½ teaspoon maple syrup
- 2 teaspoons olive oil or avocado oil

Directions:
1. Preheat the air-fryer to 180°C/350°F.
2. Chop the cauliflower into florets with a head size of roughly 5 cm/1 in. Place the other ingredients in a bowl and mix together, then add the florets and toss to coat them.
3. Add the cauliflower to the preheated air-fryer and air-fry for 12 minutes, shaking the drawer a couple of times during cooking.

Hasselback New Potatoes

Servings: 4

Ingredients:
- 8–12 new potatoes, roughly 5–7 cm/2–2¾ in. in length
- 2 teaspoons olive oil
- salt
- 1 tablespoon butter (optional)

Directions:
1. Preheat the air-fryer to 180°C/350°F.
2. Slice the potatoes multiple times widthways, making sure you do not cut all the way through (if you place the potatoes in the bowl of a wooden spoon to make these slices, it prevents you cutting all the way through). Coat the potatoes in the olive oil and sprinkle over the salt.
3. Add the potatoes to the preheated air-fryer and air-fry for 20–25 minutes until the potatoes are crispy on the outside but soft on the inside. Serve immediately.

Lentil Burgers

Servings: 4

Ingredients:
- 100g black buluga lentils
- 1 carrot, grated
- 1 diced onion
- 100g white cabbage
- 300g oats
- 1 tbsp garlic puree
- 1 tsp cumin
- Salt and pepper

Directions:
1. Blend the oats until they resemble flour
2. Put the lentils in a pan with water and cook for 45 minutes
3. Steam your vegetables for 5 minutes
4. Add all the ingredients into a bowl and mix well to combine
5. Form into burgers place in the air fryer and cook at 180ºC for 30 minutes

Roasted Brussels Sprouts

Servings: 3

Ingredients:
- 300 g/10½ oz. Brussels sprouts, trimmed and halved
- 1 tablespoon olive oil
- ½ teaspoon salt
- ¼ teaspoon freshly ground black pepper

Directions:
1. Preheat the air-fryer to 160ºC/325ºF.
2. Toss the Brussels sprout halves in the oil and the seasoning. Add these to the preheated air-fryer and air-fry for 15 minutes, then increase the temperature of the air-fryer to 180ºC/350ºF and cook for a further 5 minutes until the sprouts are really crispy on the outside and cooked through.

Roasted Cauliflower

Servings: 2

Ingredients:
- 3 cloves garlic
- 1 tbsp peanut oil
- ½ tsp salt
- ½ tsp paprika
- 400g cauliflower florets

Directions:
1. Preheat air fryer to 200ºC
2. Crush the garlic, place all ingredients in a bowl and mix well
3. Place in the air fryer and cook for about 15 minutes, shaking every 5 minutes

Two-step Pizza

Servings: 1

Ingredients:
- BASE
- 130 g/generous ½ cup Greek yogurt
- 125 g self-raising/self-rising flour, plus extra for dusting
- ¼ teaspoon salt
- PIZZA SAUCE
- 100 g/3½ oz. passata/strained tomatoes
- 1 teaspoon dried oregano
- ¼ teaspoon garlic salt
- TOPPINGS
- 75 g/2½ oz. mozzarella, torn
- fresh basil leaves, to garnish

Directions:
1. Mix together the base ingredients in a bowl. Once the mixture starts to look crumbly, use your hands to bring the dough together into a ball. Transfer to a piece of floured parchment paper and roll to about 5 mm/¼ in. thick. Transfer to a second piece of non-floured parchment paper.
2. Preheat the air-fryer to 200ºC/400ºF.
3. Meanwhile, mix the pizza sauce ingredients together in a small bowl and set aside.
4. Prick the pizza base all over with a fork and transfer (on the parchment paper) to the preheated air-fryer and air-fry for 5 minutes. Turn the pizza base over and top with the pizza sauce and the torn mozzarella. Cook for a further 3–4 minutes, until the cheese has melted. Serve immediately with the basil scattered over the top.

Bbq Soy Curls

Servings: 2

Ingredients:
- 250ml warm water
- 1 tsp vegetable bouillon
- 200g soy curls
- 40g BBQ sauce
- 1 tsp oil

Directions:
1. Soak the soy curls in water and bouillon for 10 minutes
2. Place the soy curls in another bowl and shred
3. Heat the air fryer to 200°C
4. Cook for 3 minutes
5. Remove from the air fryer and coat in bbq sauce
6. Return to the air fryer and cook for 5 minutes shaking halfway through

Vegetarian Air Fryer Kimchi Bun

Servings: 4
Cooking Time: 20 Mints

Ingredients:
- 1300 g pack of Quorn Mince
- 1/2 cup chopped kimchi, save a splash of kimchi juice
- 2-3 chopped spring onions
- 1 egg
- 1 tbsp sesame oil
- 1 tbsp soy sauce
- 1 tsp white pepper powder
- Pinch of salt
- For the dough:
- 480 g flour
- 260 ml warm water
- 2 g salt

Directions:
1. Combine all the dough ingredients in a large bowl, mix well and shape into a ball. Let the dough rest for 10 minutes before kneading for 5 minutes and then resting for a further hour.
2. Mix all the remaining ingredients together, ensuring all liquid has been well absorbed by the Quorn Mince.
3. Lay out the dough on a lightly floured surface and cut into 16 equal pieces (about 30g/piece).
4. Wrap an equal amount of filling into each piece of dough, using your hands to form into a smooth and tightly wrapped bun.
5. Preheat air fryer to 180°C/350°F Place the buns into the air fryer and spray some oil over the top of each bun, cook for 10-15 mins until golden and enjoy!

Roast Vegetables

Servings: 4

Ingredients:
- 100g diced courgette
- 100g diced squash
- 100g diced mushrooms
- 100g diced cauliflower
- 100g diced asparagus
- 100g diced pepper
- 2 tsp oil
- ½ tsp salt
- ¼ tsp pepper
- ¼ tsp seasoning

Directions:
1. Preheat air fryer to 180°C
2. Mix all ingredients together
3. Add to air fryer and cook for 10 minutes stirring halfway

Honey Roasted Parsnips

Servings: 4

Ingredients:
- 350 g/12 oz. parsnips
- 1 tablespoon plain/all-purpose flour (gluten-free if you wish)
- 1½ tablespoons runny honey
- 2 tablespoons olive oil
- salt

Directions:
1. Top and tail the parsnips, then slice lengthways, about 2 cm/¾ in. wide. Place in a saucepan with water to cover and a good pinch of salt. Bring to the boil, then boil for 5 minutes.
2. Remove and drain well, allowing any excess water to evaporate. Dust the parsnips with flour. Mix together the honey and oil in a small bowl, then toss in the parsnips to coat well in the honey and oil.
3. Preheat the air-fryer to 180°C/350°F.
4. Add the parsnips to the preheated air-fryer and air-fry for 14–16 minutes, depending on how dark you like the outsides (the longer you cook them, the sweeter they get).

Pakoras

Servings: 8

Ingredients:
- 200g chopped cauliflower
- 100g diced pepper
- 250g chickpea flour
- 30ml water
- ½ tsp cumin
- Cooking spray
- 1 onion, diced
- 1 tsp salt
- 1 garlic clove, minced
- 1 tsp curry powder
- 1 tsp coriander
- ½ tsp cayenne

Directions:
1. Preheat air fryer to 175°C
2. Place all ingredients in a bowl and mix well
3. Spray cooking basket with oil
4. Spoon 2 tbsp of mix into the basket and flatten, continue until the basket is full
5. Cook for 8 minutes, turn then cook for a further 8 minutes

Baked Potato

Servings: 1

Ingredients:
- 1 large potato
- 1 tsp oil
- ¼ tsp onion powder
- ⅛ tsp coarse salt
- 1 tbsp of butter
- 1 tbsp of cream cheese
- 1 strip of bacon, diced
- 1 tbsp olives
- 1 tbsp chives

Directions:
1. Pierce the potato in several places with a fork, rub with oil, salt and onion powder
2. Place in the air fryer and cook at 200°C for 35-40 minutes
3. Remove from the air fryer, cut and top with the toppings

Miso Mushrooms On Sourdough Toast

Servings: 1

Ingredients:
- 1 teaspoon miso paste
- 1 teaspoon oil, such as avocado or coconut (melted)
- 1 teaspoon soy sauce
- 80 g/3 oz. chestnut mushrooms, sliced 5 mm/½ in. thick
- 1 large slice sourdough bread
- 2 teaspoons butter or plant-based spread
- a little freshly chopped flat-leaf parsley, to serve

Directions:
1. Preheat the air-fryer to 200°C/400°F.
2. In a small bowl or ramekin mix together the miso paste, oil and soy sauce.
3. Place the mushrooms in a small shallow gratin dish that fits inside your air-fryer. Add the sauce to the mushrooms and mix together. Place the gratin dish in the preheated air-fryer and air-fry for 6–7 minutes, stirring once during cooking.
4. With 4 minutes left to cook, add the bread to the air-fryer and turn over at 2 minutes whilst giving the mushrooms a final stir.
5. Once cooked, butter the toast and serve the mushrooms on top, scattered with chopped parsley.

Flat Mushroom Pizzas

Servings: 1

Ingredients:
- 2 portobello mushrooms, cleaned and stalk removed
- 6 mozzarella balls
- 1 teaspoon olive oil
- PIZZA SAUCE
- 100 g/3½ oz. passata/strained tomatoes
- 1 teaspoon dried oregano
- ¼ teaspoon garlic salt

Directions:
1. Preheat the air-fryer to 180°C/350°F.
2. Mix the ingredients for the pizza sauce together in a small bowl. Fill each upturned portobello mushroom with sauce, then top each with three mozzarella balls and drizzle the olive oil over.
3. Add the mushrooms to the preheated air-fryer and air-fry for 8 minutes. Serve immediately.

Air Fryer Carrots Recipes

Servings: 2
Cooking Time: 15 Mints

Ingredients:
- 227 g carrots, peeled
- 2 teaspoons olive oil
- 1 teaspoon dried herbs (thyme, basil, mint, etc.)
- 1/2 teaspoon kosher salt, or to taste
- Black pepper, to taste

Directions:
1. Wash the fresh carrots. Slice the carrots diagonally in 1/2-inch thick slices. Combine the olive oil, herbs, salt & pepper in a bowl. Add the carrots and toss to evenly combine. Place the carrots in the air fryer basket.
2. Air Fry at 360°F/180°C for 10-15 minutes or until your desired texture.

Vegan Fried Ravioli

Servings: 4

Ingredients:
- 100g panko breadcrumbs
- 2 tsp yeast
- 1 tsp basil
- 1 tsp oregano
- 1 tsp garlic powder
- Pinch salt and pepper
- 50ml liquid from can of chickpeas
- 150g vegan ravioli
- Cooking spray
- 50g marinara for dipping

Directions:
1. Combine the breadcrumbs, yeast, basil, oregano, garlic powder and salt and pepper
2. Put the liquid from the chickpeas in a bowl
3. Dip the ravioli in the liquid then dip into the breadcrumb mix
4. Heat the air fryer to 190°C
5. Place the ravioli in the air fryer and cook for about 6 minutes until crispy

Quinoa-stuffed Romano Peppers

Servings: 2

Ingredients:
- 1 tablespoon olive oil
- 1 onion, diced
- 1 garlic clove, chopped
- 100 g/⅔ cup uncooked quinoa
- 1½ tablespoons fajita seasoning
- 140 g/1 cup canned sweetcorn/corn kernels (drained weight)
- 3 romano peppers, sliced lengthways, seeds removed but stalk left intact
- 60 g/⅔ cup grated mature Cheddar

Directions:
1. Heat the oil in a saucepan. Add the onion and garlic and sauté for 5 minutes, until soft. Add the quinoa, fajita seasoning and 250 ml/1 cup water. Bring to a simmer, then cover with a lid and simmer for 15 minutes or until the quinoa is cooked and the water absorbed. Stir in the sweetcorn/corn kernels. Stuff each pepper half with the quinoa mixture, then top with grated cheese.
2. Preheat the air-fryer to 180°C/350°F.
3. Place the peppers on an air-fryer liner or a piece of pierced parchment paper, place in the preheated air-fryer and air-fry for 12–14 minutes, depending how 'chargrilled' you like your peppers.

Air Fryer Cheese Sandwich

Servings: 2
Cooking Time: 10 Minutes

Ingredients:
- 4 slices white or wholemeal bread
- 2 tbsp butter
- 50 g / 3.5 oz cheddar cheese, grated

Directions:
1. Preheat the air fryer to 180 °C / 350 °F and line the bottom of the basket with parchment paper.
2. Lay the slices of bread out on a clean surface and butter one side of each. Evenly sprinkle the cheese on two of the slices and cover with the final two slices.
3. Transfer the sandwiches to the air fryer, close the lid, and cook for 5 minutes until the bread is crispy and golden, and the cheese is melted.

Air Fryer Muchrooms

Servings: 2
Cooking Time: 35 Mints
Ingredients:
- 4 large flat mushrooms
- 2 tsp chopped fresh tarragon
- 50 g garlic butter, chopped
- Select all ingredients

Directions:
1. Heat air fryer to 180°C/350°F. Place the mushrooms, base-side up, in the air fryer basket. Sprinkle with fresh tarragon. Spray with oil and place the garlic butter on the gills of the mushrooms. Cook for 5 minutes.

Broccoli Cheese

Servings: 2
Ingredients:
- 250g broccoli
- Cooking spray
- 10 tbsp evaporated milk
- 300g Mexican cheese
- 4 tsp Amarillo paste
- 6 saltine crackers

Directions:
1. Heat the air fryer to 190°C
2. Place the broccoli in the air fryer spray with cooking oil and cook for about 6 minutes
3. Place the remaining ingredients in a blender and process until smooth
4. Place in a bowl and microwave for 30 seconds
5. Pour over the broccoli and serve

Spanakopita Bites

Servings: 4

Ingredients:
- 300g baby spinach
- 2 tbsp water
- 100g cottage cheese
- 50g feta cheese
- 2 tbsp grated parmesan
- 1 tbsp olive oil
- 4 sheets of filo pastry
- 1 large egg white
- 1 tsp lemon zest
- 1 tsp oregano
- ¼ tsp salt
- ¼ tsp pepper
- ⅛ tsp cayenne

Directions:
1. Place spinach in water and cook for about 5 minutes, drain
2. Mix all ingredients together
3. Place a sheet of pastry down and brush with oil, place another on the top and do the same, continue until all four on top of each other
4. Ut the pastry into 8 strips then cut each strip in half across the middle
5. Add 1 tbsp of mix to each piece of pastry
6. Fold one corner over the mix to create a triangle, fold over the other corner to seal
7. Place in the air fryer and cook at 190°C for about 12 minutes until golden brown

Desserts Recipes

Banana Bread

Servings: 8

Ingredients:
- 200g flour
- 1 tsp cinnamon
- ½ tsp salt
- ¼ tsp baking soda
- 2 ripe banana mashed
- 2 large eggs
- 75g sugar
- 25g plain yogurt
- 2 tbsp oil
- 1 tsp vanilla extract
- 2 tbsp chopped walnuts
- Cooking spray

Directions:
1. Line a 6 inch cake tin with parchment paper and coat with cooking spray
2. Whisk together flour, cinnamon, salt and baking soda set aside
3. In another bowl mix together remaining ingredients, add the flour mix and combine well
4. Pour batter into the cake tin and place in the air fryer
5. Cook at 155°C for 35 minutes turning halfway through

Key Lime Cupcakes

Servings: 6

Ingredients:
- 250g Greek yogurt
- 200g soft cheese
- 2 eggs
- Juice and rind of 2 limes
- 1 egg yolk
- ¼ cup caster sugar
- 1 tsp vanilla essence

Directions:
1. Mix the Greek yogurt and soft cheese together until smooth
2. Add the eggs and mix, add the lime juice, rind, vanilla and caster sugar and mix well
3. Fill 6 cupcake cases with the mix and place the rest to one side
4. Place in the air fryer and cook at 160°C for 10 minutes then another 10 minutes at 180°C
5. Place the remaining mix into a piping bag, once the cupcakes have cooled pipe on the top and place in the fridge to set

Cherry Pies

Servings: 6

Ingredients:
- 300g prepared shortcrust pastry
- 75g cherry pie filling
- Cooking spray
- 3 tbsp icing sugar
- ½ tsp milk

Directions:
1. Cut out 6 pies with a cookie cutter
2. Add 1 ½ tbsp filling to each pie
3. Fold the dough in half and seal around the edges with a fork
4. Place in the air fryer, spray with cooking spray
5. Cook at 175°C for 10 minutes
6. Mix icing sugar and milk and drizzled over cooled pies to serve

Chonut Holes

Servings: 12

Ingredients:
- 225g flour
- 75g sugar
- 1 tsp baking powder
- ¼ tsp cinnamon
- 2 tbsp sugar
- ½ tsp salt
- 2 tbsp aquafaba
- 1 tbsp melted coconut oil
- 75ml soy milk
- 2 tsp cinnamon

Directions:
1. In a bowl mix the flour, ¼ cup sugar, baking powder, ¼ tsp cinnamon and salt
2. Add the aquafaba, coconut oil and soy milk mix well
3. In another bowl mix 2 tsp cinnamon and 2 tbsp sugar
4. Line the air fryer with parchment paper
5. Divide the dough into 12 pieces and dredge with the cinnamon sugar mix
6. Place in the air fryer at 185°C and cook for 6-8 minutes, don't shake them

Christmas Biscuits

Servings: 8

Ingredients:
- 225g self raising flour
- 100g caster sugar
- 100g butter
- Juice and rind of orange
- 1 egg beaten
- 2 tbsp cocoa
- 2 tsp vanilla essence
- 8 pieces dark chocolate

Directions:
1. Preheat the air fryer to 180°C
2. Rub the butter into the flour. Add the sugar, vanilla, orange and cocoa mix well
3. Add the egg and mix to a dough
4. Split the dough into 8 equal pieces
5. Place a piece of chocolate in each piece of dough and form into a ball covering the chocolate
6. Place in the air fryer and cook for 15 minutes

Fried Oreos

Servings: 8

Ingredients:
- 1 tube crescent rolls
- 8 Oreos

Directions:
1. Wrap the Oreos in the crescent roll dough, trim off any excess
2. Spray the air fryer with cooking spray
3. Place Oreos in the air fryer and cook at 175ºC for 6 minutes

Thai Fried Bananas

Servings: 8

Ingredients:
- 4 ripe bananas
- 2 tbsp flour
- 2 tbsp rice flour
- 2 tbsp cornflour
- 2 tbsp desiccated coconut
- Pinch salt
- ½ tsp baking powder
- ½ tsp cardamon powder

Directions:
1. Place all the dry ingredients in a bowl and mix well. Add a little water at a time and combine to form a batter
2. Cut the bananas in half and then half again length wise
3. Line the air fryer with parchment paper and spray with cooking spray
4. Dip each banana piece in the batter mix and place in the air fryer
5. Cook at 200ºC for 10 -15 minutes turning halfway
6. Serve with ice cream

White Chocolate And Raspberry Loaf

Servings: 8
Cooking Time: 1 Hour 10 Minutes

Ingredients:

- 400 g / 14 oz plain flour
- 2 tsp baking powder
- 1 tsp ground cinnamon
- ½ tsp salt
- 3 eggs, beaten
- 50 g / 3.5 oz granulated sugar
- 50 g / 3.5 oz brown sugar
- 100 g / 3.5 oz white chocolate chips
- 100 g / 3.5 oz fresh raspberries
- 1 tbsp cocoa powder
- 4 tbsp milk
- 1 tsp vanilla extract

Directions:

1. Preheat the air fryer to 150 °C / 300 °F and line a loaf tin with parchment paper.
2. Combine the plain flour, baking powder, ground cinnamon, and salt in a large mixing bowl.
3. Whisk eggs into the bowl, then stir in the granulated sugar and brown sugar. Mix well before folding in the white chocolate chips, fresh raspberries, cocoa powder, milk, and vanilla extract.
4. Stir the mixture until it is lump-free and transfer into a lined loaf tin. Place the loaf tin into the lined air fryer basket, close the lid, and cook for 30-40 minutes.
5. The cake should be golden and set by the end of the cooking process. Insert a knife into the centre of the cake. It should come out dry when the cake is fully cooked.
6. Remove the cake from the air fryer, still in the loaf tin. Set aside to cool on a drying rack for 20-30 minutes before cutting into slices and serving.

Chocolate-glazed Banana Slices

Servings: 2
Cooking Time: 10 Minutes

Ingredients:

- 2 bananas
- 1 tbsp honey
- 1 tbsp chocolate spread, melted
- 2 tbsp milk chocolate chips

Directions:

1. Preheat the air fryer to 180 °C / 350 °F. Remove the mesh basket from the machine and line it with parchment paper.
2. Cut the two bananas into even slices and place them in the lined air fryer basket.
3. In a small bowl, mix the honey and melted chocolate spread. Use a brush to glaze the banana slices. Carefully press the milk chocolate chips into the banana slices enough so that they won't fall out when you transfer the bananas into the air fryer.
4. Carefully slide the mesh basket into the air fryer, close the lid, and cook for 10 minutes until the bananas are hot and the choc chips have melted.
5. Enjoy the banana slices on their own or with a side of ice cream.

Chocolate Dipped Biscuits

Servings: 6
Ingredients:
- 225g self raising flour
- 100g sugar
- 100g butter
- 50g milk chocolate
- 1 egg beaten
- 1 tsp vanilla essence

Directions:
1. Add the flour, butter and sugar to a bowl and rub together
2. Add the egg and vanilla, mix to form a dough
3. Split the dough into 6 and form into balls
4. Place in the air fryer cook at 180°C for 15 minutes
5. Melt the chocolate, dip the cooked biscuits into the chocolate and half cover

Melting Moments

Servings: 9
Ingredients:
- 100g butter
- 75g caster sugar
- 150g self raising flour
- 1 egg
- 50g white chocolate
- 3 tbsp desiccated coconut
- 1 tsp vanilla essence

Directions:
1. Preheat the air fryer to 180°C
2. Cream together the butter and sugar, beat in the egg and vanilla
3. Bash the white chocolate into small pieces
4. Add the flour and chocolate and mix well
5. Roll into 9 small balls and cover in coconut
6. Place in the air fryer and cook for 8 minutes and a further 6 minutes at 160°C

Zebra Cake

Servings: 6

Ingredients:
- 115g butter
- 2 eggs
- 100g caster sugar
- 1 tbsp cocoa powder
- 100g self raising flour
- 30ml milk
- 1tsp vanilla

Directions:
1. Preheat air fryer to 160ºC
2. Line a 6 inch baking tin
3. Beat together the butter and sugar until light and fluffy
4. Add eggs one at a time then add the vanilla and milk
5. Add the flour and mix well
6. Divide the mix in half
7. Add cocoa powder to half the mix and mix well
8. Add a scoop of each of the batters at a time until it's all in the tin, place in the air fryer and cook for 30 minutes

Pecan & Molasses Flapjack

Servings:9

Ingredients:
- 120 g/½ cup plus 2 teaspoons butter or plant-based spread, plus extra for greasing
- 40 g/2 tablespoons blackstrap molasses
- 60 g/5 tablespoons unrefined sugar
- 50 g/½ cup chopped pecans
- 200 g/1½ cups porridge oats/steelcut oats (not rolled or jumbo)

Directions:
1. Preheat the air-fryer to 180ºC/350ºF.
2. Grease and line a 15 x 15-cm/6 x 6-in. baking pan.
3. In a large saucepan melt the butter/spread, molasses and sugar. Once melted, stir in the pecans, then the oats. As soon as they are combined, tip the mixture into the prepared baking pan and cover with foil.
4. Place the foil-covered baking pan in the preheated air-fryer and air-fry for 10 minutes. Remove the foil, then cook for a further 2 minutes to brown the top. Leave to cool, then cut into 9 squares.

Lava Cakes

Servings: 4

Ingredients:

- 1 ½ tbsp self raising flour
- 3 ½ tbsp sugar
- 150g butter
- 150g dark chocolate, chopped
- 2 eggs

Directions:

1. Preheat the air fryer to 175°C
2. Grease 4 ramekin dishes
3. Melt chocolate and butter in the microwave for about 3 minutes
4. Whisk the eggs and sugar together until pale and frothy
5. Pour melted chocolate into the eggs and stir in the flour
6. Fill the ramekins ¾ full, place in the air fryer and cook for 10 minutes

French Toast Sticks

Servings: 12

Ingredients:

- 2 eggs
- 25g milk
- 1 tbsp melted butter
- 1 tsp vanilla extract
- 1 tsp cinnamon
- 4 slices bread, cut into thirds
- 1 tsp icing sugar

Directions:

1. Mix eggs, milk, butter, vanilla and cinnamon together in a bowl
2. Line the air fryer with parchment paper
3. Dip each piece of bread into the egg mixture
4. Place in the air fryer and cook at 190°C for 6 minutes, turn over and cook for another 3 minutes
5. Sprinkle with icing sugar to serve

Brownies

Servings: 6

Ingredients:
- 25g melted butter
- 50g sugar
- 1 egg
- ½ tsp vanilla
- 25g flour
- 3 tbsp cocoa
- ⅛ tsp baking powder
- ⅛ tsp salt

Directions:
1. Preheat the air fryer to 165°C
2. Add all the wet ingredients to a bowl and combine.
3. Add the dry ingredients and mix well
4. Place the batter into a prepared pan and cook in the air fryer for 13 minutes

Mini Egg Buns

Servings: 8

Ingredients:
- 100g self raising flour
- 100g caster sugar
- 100g butter
- 2 eggs
- 2 tbsp honey
- 1 tbsp vanilla essence
- 300g soft cheese
- 100g icing sugar
- 2 packets of Mini Eggs

Directions:
1. Cream the butter and sugar together until light and fluffy, beat in the eggs one at a time
2. Add the honey and vanilla essence, fold in the flour a bit at a time
3. Divide the mix into 8 bun cases and place in the air fryer. Cook at 180°C for about 20 minutes
4. Cream the soft cheese and icing sugar together to make the topping
5. Allow the buns to cool, pipe on the topping mix and add mini eggs

Lemon Buns

Servings: 12

Ingredients:

- 100g butter
- 100g caster sugar
- 2 eggs
- 100g self raising flour
- ½ tsp vanilla essence
- 1 tsp cherries
- 50g butter
- 100g icing sugar
- ½ small lemon rind and juice

Directions:

1. Preheat the air fryer to 170ºC
2. Cream the 100g butter, sugar and vanilla together until light and fluffy
3. Beat in the eggs one at a time adding a little flour with each
4. Fold in the remaining flour
5. Half fill bun cases with the mix, place in the air fryer and cook for 8 minutes
6. Cream 50g butter then mix in the icing sugar, stir in the lemon
7. Slice the top off each bun and create a butterfly shape using the icing to hold together. Add a 1/3 cherry to each one

Strawberry Danish

Servings: 2

Ingredients:

- 1 tube crescent roll dough
- 200g cream cheese
- 25g strawberry jam
- 50g diced strawberries
- 225g powdered sugar
- 2-3 tbsp cream

Directions:

1. Roll out the dough
2. Spread the cream cheese over the dough, cover in jam
3. Sprinkle with strawberries
4. Roll the dough up from the short side and pinch to seal
5. Line the air fryer with parchment paper and spray with cooking spray
6. Place the dough in the air fryer and cook at 175ºC for 20 minutes
7. Mix the cream with the powdered sugar and drizzle on top once cooked

Chocolate Orange Muffins

Servings: 12

Ingredients:
- 100g self raising flour
- 110g caster sugar
- 50g butter
- 20g cocoa powder
- 50ml milk
- 1 tsp cocoa nibs
- 1 large orange juice and rind
- 1 tbsp honey
- 1tsp vanilla essence
- 2 eggs

Directions:
1. Add the flour, butter and sugar to a mixing bowl and rug together
2. Add the cocoa, honey, orange and vanilla mix well
3. Mix the milk and egg together then add to the flour mix, combine well
4. Rub your muffin cases with flour to stop them sticking, add 2 tbsp batter to each one
5. Cook in the air fryer for 12 minutes at 180ºC

Grilled Ginger & Coconut Pineapple Rings

Servings: 4

Ingredients:
- 1 medium pineapple
- coconut oil, melted
- 1½ teaspoons coconut sugar
- ½ teaspoon ground ginger
- coconut or vanilla yogurt, to serve

Directions:
1. Preheat the air-fryer to 180ºC/350ºF.
2. Peel and core the pineapple, then slice into 4 thick rings.
3. Mix together the melted coconut oil with the sugar and ginger in a small bowl. Using a pastry brush, paint this mixture all over the pineapple rings, including the sides of the rings.
4. Add the rings to the preheated air-fryer and air-fry for 20 minutes. Check after 18 minutes as pineapple sizes vary and your rings may be perfectly cooked already. You'll know they are ready when they're golden in colour and a fork can easily be inserted with very little resistance
5. Serve warm with a generous spoonful of yogurt.

Recipe Index

A

Alba Salad With Air Fried Butterfly Shrimp 56

Air Fryer Breaded Pork Chops 49

Air Fryer Boiled Eggs 25

Air Fryer Cheese Sandwich 79

Air Fryer Chicken Parmesan 35

Air Fryer Chicken Wings 37

Air Fryer Chicken Strips 39

Air Fryer Crispy Chickpeas 26

Air Fryer Carrots Recipes 78

Air Fryer Corn On The Cob 68

Air Fryer French Bread Pizza (homemade) 23

Air Fryer Frozen Chicken Cordon Bleu 29

Air Fryer Garlic Herb Turkey Breast 31

Air Fryer Hunters Chicken 35

Air Fryer Hot Dogs 22

Air Fryer Lemon Pepper Shrimp 57

Air Fryer Muchrooms 80

Air Fryer Pork Bratwurst 42

Air Fryer Roast Pork Belly 41

Air Fryer Tuna 60

Air Fryer Tuna Mornay Parcels 53

Air Fryer Turkey Avocado Burgers 18

Air Fryer Eggy Bread 67

Air Fryer Spicy Bay Scallops 53

Air Fryer Stuffed Zucchini Boats With Sausage 20

Air Fryer Salmon Fillets 58

Air Fried Fish Tostadas With Mango Salsa 59

B

Bbq Beetroot Crisps 64

Bbq Soy Curls 74

Breakfast "pop Tarts" 15

Broccoli Cheese 80

Brownies 89

Buffalo Chicken Wontons 30

Buffalo Wings 28

Butter Steak & Asparagus 43

Baked Potato 76

Banana Bread 81

Beef Nacho Pinwheels 45

Beef Wellington 48

Beetroot Crisps 22

C

Christmas Biscuits 83

Char Siu Buffalo 39

Cheddar & Bbq Stuffed Chicken 34

Cherry Pies 82

Cheesy Meatball Sub 46

Cheesy Taco Crescents 25

Chicken & Bacon Parcels 21

Chicken Fried Rice 36

Chicken Tikka Masala 38

Chicken And Cheese Chimichangas 30

Chicken And Wheat Stir Fry 36

Chilli Lime Tilapia 51

Chinese Chilli Beef 48

Chocolate Dipped Biscuits 86

Chocolate Orange Muffins 91

Chocolate-glazed Banana Slices 85

Chonut Holes 83

Crunchy Mexican Breakfast Wrap 16

Crispy Cajun Fish Fingers 52

Crispy Cinnamon French Toast 67

Crispy Sweet & Spicy Cauliflower 71

Cumin Shoestring Carrots 24

Cajun Prawn Skewers 61

Cajun Shrimp Boil 60

Copycat Burger 41

Copycat Fish Fingers 52

Corn Nuts 27

Courgette Gratin 70

D

Delicious Breakfast Casserole 14

E

Egg & Bacon Breakfast Cups 16

Egg Fried Rice 65

European Pancakes 14

Extra Crispy Popcorn Shrimp 56

Easy Cheese & Bacon Toasties 12

Easy Omelette 15

F

Flat Mushroom Pizzas 77

French Toast Sticks 88

Fried Oreos 84

G

Grilled Bacon And Cheese 63

Grilled Ginger & Coconut Pineapple Rings 91

Garlic Butter Salmon 54

Garlic Cheese Bread 27

Garlic Parmesan Fried Chicken Wings 37

Garlic And Parsley Potatoes 61

H

Hamburgers 43

Hard Boiled Eggs Air Fryer Style 13

Hasselback New Potatoes 71

Healthy Air Fryer Herbed Turkey Breast With Lemon Pepper 32

Healthy Stuffed Peppers 12

Homemade Crispy Pepperoni Pizza 40

Honey & Mustard Meatballs 49

Honey Cajun Chicken Thighs 29

Honey Roasted Parsnips 75

Honey Sriracha Salmon 59

J

Japanese Pork Chops 47

K

Key Lime Cupcakes 82

L

Lava Cakes 88

Lemon Buns 90

Lentil Burgers 72

M

Muhammara 28

Mustard Pork Tenderloin 47

Mediterranean Beef Meatballs 42

Melting Moments 86

Mexican Breakfast Burritos 17

Mexican Rice 68

Mini Egg Buns 89

Miso Mushrooms On Sourdough Toast 77

N

Nashville Chicken 32

O

Olive Stained Turkey Breast 34

Orange Sesame Cauliflower 64

P

Pumpkin Fries 69

Pakoras 76

Parmesan Crusted Pork Chops 40

Pecan & Molasses Flapjack 87

Pepper & Lemon Chicken Wings 33

Peppery Lemon Shrimp 50

Popcorn Tofu 20

Pork Chilli Cheese Dogs 45

Pork Jerky 23

Pork Taquitos 50

Potato Fries 24

Potato Wedges 63

Potato Wedges With Rosemary 66

Q

Quinoa-stuffed Romano Peppers 79

R

Radish Hash Browns 70

Roast Vegetables 75

Roasted Brussels Sprouts 72

Roasted Cauliflower 73

Roasted Almonds 19

Roasted Okra 69

S

Shishito Peppers 66

Smoky Chicken Breast 38

Spanakopita Bites 81

Strawberry Danish 90

Stuffed Jacket Potatoes 65

Sticky Chicken Tikka Drumsticks 33

Store-cupboard Fishcakes 58

Swede Fries 21

Sweet Potato Fries 17

Sweet Potato Tots 62

Salmon Patties 55

Salt & Pepper Calamari 54

Salt And Pepper Belly Pork 44

Sea Bass With Asparagus Spears 55

T

Thai Fried Bananas 84

Turkey Cutlets In Mushroom Sauce 31

Two-step Pizza 73

Tandoori Salmon 57

Tangy Breakfast Hash 13

Tender Ham Steaks 44

Tilapia Fillets 51

U

Ultra Crispy Air Fryer Chickpeas 18

V

Vegan Fried Ravioli 78

Vegetable & Beef Frittata 46

Vegetarian Air Fryer Kimchi Bun 74

W

White Chocolate And Raspberry Loaf 85

Wholegrain Pitta Chips 26

Z

Zebra Cake 87

Zingy Roasted Carrots 62

Printed in Great Britain
by Amazon